SpringerBriefs in Computer Science

SpringerBriefs present concise summaries of cutting-edge research and practical applications across a wide spectrum of fields. Featuring compact volumes of 50 to 125 pages, the series covers a range of content from professional to academic.

Typical topics might include:

- A timely report of state-of-the art analytical techniques
- A bridge between new research results, as published in journal articles, and a contextual literature review
- A snapshot of a hot or emerging topic
- An in-depth case study or clinical example
- A presentation of core concepts that students must understand in order to make independent contributions

Briefs allow authors to present their ideas and readers to absorb them with minimal time investment. Briefs will be published as part of Springer's eBook collection, with millions of users worldwide. In addition, Briefs will be available for individual print and electronic purchase. Briefs are characterized by fast, global electronic dissemination, standard publishing contracts, easy-to-use manuscript preparation and formatting guidelines, and expedited production schedules. We aim for publication 8–12 weeks after acceptance. Both solicited and unsolicited manuscripts are considered for publication in this series.

**Indexing: This series is indexed in Scopus, Ei-Compendex, and zbMATH **

Weidang Lu • Yu Ding • Huimei Han • Guanjun Xu

Secure Communications in Unmanned Aerial Vehicle-Enabled Mobile Edge Computing Systems

Weidang Lu
College of Information Engineering
Zhejiang University of Technology
Hangzhou, China

Yu Ding
College of Information Engineering
Zhejiang University of Technology
Hangzhou, China

Huimei Han
College of Information Engineering
Zhejiang University of Technology
Hangzhou, China

Guanjun Xu
Space Information Research Institute
Hangzhou Dianzi University
Hangzhou, China

ISSN 2191-5768 ISSN 2191-5776 (electronic)
SpringerBriefs in Computer Science
ISBN 978-981-96-9610-9 ISBN 978-981-96-9611-6 (eBook)
https://doi.org/10.1007/978-981-96-9611-6

This Springer imprint is published by the registered company Springer Nature Singapore Pte Ltd.
The registered company address is: 152 Beach Road, #21-01/04 Gateway East, Singapore 189721, Singapore

Preface

The rapid growth of modern IoT applications has resulted in an explosive rise in connected devices and generated data. Around half of these devices struggle with stable connectivity and efficient data transmission due to limited network capacity, severely hindering communication performance and service quality in large-scale deployments. This highlights the urgent demand for innovative frameworks capable of managing dynamic, resource-intensive workloads with lower latency and higher efficiency. UAV-enabled MEC systems present a promising solution to these challenges. By leveraging the mobility and rapid deployment of UAVs alongside the localized computing capabilities of MEC, these systems support efficient task offloading, enhanced computational performance, and real-time data handling. However, despite these benefits, UAV-MEC systems face significant security issues stemming from the open and broadcast nature of wireless communication. Thus in this brief, we focus on the secure communication in UAV-enabled MEC system to address these threats.

In Chap. 1, we start by providing an overview of UAV-MEC systems and fundamentals of secure communication. To demonstrate secure communication designs in UAV-enabled MEC systems, we present two specific examples and highlight their potential advantages in Chaps. 2–4. Specifically, in Chap. 2, we study the PLS techniques tailored for UAV-enabled MEC systems and examine how the inherent features of wireless communication channels and transmission methods can be leveraged to ensure robust security in data transmission. Moreover, two secure communication schemes based on TDMA and NOMA are proposed. In Chap. 3, we study the RIS-based secure communication for UAV-enabled MEC systems to further enhance communication and computation efficiency. Two RIS-based schemes are evaluated through simulations, demonstrating performance gains over traditional benchmarks. In Chap. 4, we study the DRL-based secure communication for UAV-enabled MEC systems to optimize task offloading decisions in dynamic environments. Two DRL-based schemes are proposed to improve system utility and reduce delay. Simulation results demonstrate that these schemes significantly outperform random offloading strategies. Finally, in Chap. 5, we conclude the study and outline potential directions for future research.

This brief illustrates the designs of the secure communication in UAV-enabled MEC system and demonstrates the associated potential advantages. This brief can be served as a textbook or reference material for postgraduate students studying advanced topics in wireless communications and MEC system.

We would like to thank Fuyuqi Zhang, Yifan Chen, Xin Chen, Mingfeng Cao, and Yandan Mo from Zhejiang University of Technology for their research contributions to the presented Springer Brief. Special thanks are due to the editors at Springer Science+Business Media, Ellen Seo, Kamesh Senthilkumar, Nick Zhu, and Cassie Peng, for their help throughout the publication preparation process.

This work is supported in part by the Zhejiang Provincial Natural Science Foundation of China under Grants LR25F010003 and LQ24F010013, in part by the National Natural Science Foundation under Grants 62271447, 62301490, 62001419, and 62131016, and in part by the Fundamental Research Funds for the Provincial Universities of Zhejiang under Grant RF-C2023008.

Hangzhou, China

Weidang Lu
Yu Ding
Huimei Han
Guanjun Xu

Declarations

Competing Interests The authors have no competing interests to declare that are relevant to the content of this manuscript.

Contents

Acronyms

5G	Fifth Generation
AWGN	Additive White Gaussian Noise
BCD	Block Coordinate Descent
BS	Base Station
CPU	Central Processing Unit
CSI	Channel State Information
DRL	Deep Reinforcement Learning
FDMA	Frequency Division Multiple Access
GJ	Ground Jammer
GU	Ground User
IoT	Internet of Things
LoS	Line-of-Sight
MDP	Markov Decision Process
MISO	Multiple Input Single Output
MEC	Mobile Edge Computing
NOMA	Non-orthogonal Multiple Access
OMA	Orthogonal Multiple Access
PLS	Physical Layer Security
RIS	Reconfigurable Intelligent Surface
SCA	Successive Convex Approximation
SIC	Successive Interference Cancellation
SINR	Signal-to-Interference-and-Noise Ratio
SNR	Signal-to-Noise Ratio
TDMA	Time Division Multiple Access
UAV	Unmanned Aerial Vehicle

Chapter 1
Overview of UAV-MEC Systems and Fundamentals of Secure Communications

The rapid advancement of modern IoT applications, such as autonomous vehicles, telemedicine, and industrial automation, has led to an unprecedented increase in the number of connected devices and the volume of data generated [1–4]. According to analyses from the IDC and Cisco, the global IoT device count has reached nearly 50 billion, exerting immense pressure on existing network and computing infrastructures. Approximately 50% of these devices face challenges in achieving stable connectivity and data transmission due to network capacity limitations, which severely restrict communication capabilities and service quality in large-scale networks. This limitation underscores the critical need for novel frameworks that can handle dynamic, resource-intensive tasks with reduced latency and improved efficiency [5–8]. UAV-MEC systems offer a transformative approach to address these challenges. By combining the mobility and rapid deployment capabilities of UAVs with the localized processing power of edge computing, UAV-MEC systems enable efficient task offloading, enhanced computational capacity, and real-time data processing. Moreover, they provide flexible and scalable solutions for supporting IoT applications in areas with limited infrastructure. Despite their advantages, UAV-MEC systems face critical security challenges due to the inherent openness and broadcast nature of wireless communication channels. LoS transmissions are especially vulnerable to interception and interference from malicious eavesdroppers. These threats not only compromise data confidentiality but also disrupt normal network operations. To mitigate these risks, secure communication strategies must be integrated into UAV-MEC frameworks.

In this chapter, we first introduce UAV-enabled MEC systems and then overview secure communications in UAV-enabled MEC systems. Next, several challenges are analyzed in secure communications in UAV-enabled MEC systems. Moreover, we discuss about open issues in secure communications in UAV-enabled MEC systems and illustrate the contributions of this brief.

W. Lu et al., *Secure Communications in Unmanned Aerial Vehicle-Enabled Mobile Edge Computing Systems*, SpringerBriefs in Computer Science,
https://doi.org/10.1007/978-981-96-9611-6_1

1.1 UAV-Enabled MEC Systems

MEC is an emerging paradigm designed to address the limitations of traditional cloud computing in latency-sensitive applications [9–12]. By relocating computational power and storage modules to network edge layers, MEC establishes a framework for task offloading from terminal devices to neighboring edge computing units, driving comprehensive performance upgrades. The minimized spatial separation between data sources and processing nodes enables accelerated computational throughput while alleviating cloud-core network burdens [13–15]. This architecture becomes operationally mandatory for autonomous driving systems, augmented reality interfaces, and IoT deployments—all requiring millisecond-level responsiveness and generating terabit-scale datasets that challenge conventional cloud-centric paradigms. However, traditional MEC systems rely heavily on fixed infrastructure, which can limit their flexibility and applicability in dynamic or infrastructure-deficient environments.

UAVs, with their mobility and adaptability, have become a powerful tool for addressing these limitations [16–18]. Equipped with advanced communication modules and edge computing servers, UAVs can act as mobile BSs or computing nodes, offering rapid deployment and dynamic positioning capabilities. UAVs excel in scenarios where traditional communication infrastructure is unavailable or insufficient, such as disaster recovery, remote regions, or temporary event networks. The ability to adjust flight trajectories in real time allows UAVs to maintain robust communication links and optimize network performance.

The convergence of MEC and UAV technologies gives rise to UAV-enabled MEC systems, a novel architecture designed to harness the benefits of both approaches [19–23]. UAV-enabled MEC systems integrate the mobility and flexibility of UAVs with the computational efficiency of MEC, enabling dynamic and distributed processing capabilities. UAVs serve as mobile edge nodes, providing dynamic and flexible network support by adjusting their positions to optimize communication links and resource allocation. UAVs can offload tasks from devices, perform local computations, and deliver low-latency services to meet the stringent requirements of various IoT applications. Moreover, UAVs' ability to provide coverage in areas without fixed infrastructure offers a cost-effective and scalable solution to expand connectivity and computing resources.

1.2 Secure Communications in UAV-Enabled MEC Systems

The integration of secure communication mechanisms is pivotal in UAV-enabled MEC systems, where data offloading, processing, and transmission occur over wireless channels susceptible to various security threats [24–28]. The openness of wireless networks, coupled with the mobility of UAVs, amplifies the risks of data interception, tampering, and disruption, necessitating robust strategies to ensure the confidentiality, integrity, and availability of transmitted information.

Key characteristics of secure communications in UAV-enabled MEC systems:

1. **Openness and vulnerability of wireless links.**
   UAVs communicate through wireless channels, which are inherently vulnerable to interception. The LoS transmission, while beneficial for maintaining strong communication links, exposes the system to eavesdroppers with direct access to the communication pathway.
2. **Mobility-induced security challenges.**
   The high mobility of UAVs and the dynamic nature of network topologies create fluctuating communication environments. These conditions make it difficult to maintain consistent security measures, as adversaries can exploit these dynamics to carry out attacks such as eavesdropping or signal interception.
3. **Resource constraints.**
   UAVs are often constrained in terms of onboard computational capacity and energy availability. The limited computational and energy resources of UAVs impose restrictions on the implementation of conventional security mechanisms. Lightweight and resources-efficient security strategies are crucial to maintaining operational feasibility.
4. **Susceptibility to active attacks.**
   UAV-enabled MEC systems are vulnerable to active attacks, which can send attacking signals to disrupt communication links. These serious threats compromise both the reliability and security of the UAV-enabled MEC system, posing significant risks to data integrity.

In summary, secure communication serves as a cornerstone for the successful operation of UAV-enabled MEC systems, addressing the unique vulnerabilities and dynamic security requirements inherent in such environments. The key characteristics, including the openness of wireless links, mobility-induced challenges, and resource constraints, underscore the need for innovative and adaptive security solutions. In the subsequent sections, we will delve deeper into the challenges faced in ensuring secure communications in UAV-enabled MEC systems and explore state-of-the-art techniques and potential solutions to mitigate these risks effectively.

1.3 Challenges in Secure Communications of UAV-Enabled MEC Systems

Despite the significant potential of UAV-enabled MEC systems, ensuring secure communications remains formidable challenges due to the inherent vulnerabilities and dynamic characteristics of these systems. Below, we outline the key challenges associated with secure communications in UAV-enabled MEC systems.

- Mitigating aerial eavesdropping. The open and broadcast nature of UAV communication makes it particularly vulnerable to eavesdropping, especially in LoS transmission scenarios. Malicious UAVs or ground-based adversaries can easily position themselves within the communication range to intercept sensitive data being offloaded from devices to UAVs. The challenge is to develop robust physical-layer security techniques, such as beamforming, artificial noise generation, or secure key distribution protocols, to protect data against such threats. Furthermore, these techniques must operate efficiently in dynamic environments, where UAV positions and adversary locations are constantly changing.
- Meeting diverse user requirements. UAV-enabled MEC systems often serve a wide array of applications, each with distinct security, computational, and communication demands. For instance, autonomous vehicles may prioritize low-latency communication with moderate security, while financial transactions may demand high confidentiality regardless of latency. This diversity necessitates the development of flexible security frameworks capable of adapting to varying user-specific requirements. The challenge lies in achieving this adaptability without excessively complicating the system design or overloading the UAV's computational and communication resources.
- Balancing security with resource optimization. UAVs are inherently resource-constrained, with limited energy, computational power, and storage capacity. Implementing advanced security measures often requires additional processing power and energy. This creates a fundamental trade-off: how to ensure high levels of security without depleting UAV resources or compromising mission duration. We should design lightweight security mechanisms and develop integrated resource optimization strategies that balance the competing demands of security, energy efficiency, and communication quality.
- Ensuring security in dynamic environments. The mobility of UAVs, coupled with the variability of network conditions, introduces significant challenges to secure communication. UAVs frequently change positions to maintain optimal connectivity or avoid obstacles, which can lead to fluctuating communication links and changing security threats. For instance, UAVs moving into areas with higher interference or closer to adversaries increase the risk of data breaches. This dynamic nature requires the development of adaptive security protocols that can respond to changes in real-time, ensuring consistent protection under varying operational conditions.

1.4 Open Issues in Secure Communications of UAV-Enabled MEC Systems

Despite recent advancements in UAV-enabled MEC systems, numerous open issues remain in the domain of secure communications, encompassing aspects such as PLS-based secure communications for UAV-enabled MEC systems, RIS-enhanced transmission security, DRL-driven adaptive mechanisms, and online real-time optimization strategies. This section provides a brief discussion of them, serving as a foundation for the subsequent chapters.

PLS-based Secure Communications for UAV-enabled MEC Systems PLS technology offers a promising avenue to counteract the threat of malicious UAVs engaging in aerial eavesdropping [29–44]. However, the development of effective PLS-based optimization mechanisms tailored to UAV-enabled MEC systems remains an open issue. UAV-enabled MEC systems often operate under diverse communication modes, such as TDMA or NOMA. Designing PLS-based mechanisms that can dynamically adapt to these modes while maintaining secure transmission is critical. For instance, ensuring that devices can securely offload data to UAVs without being intercepted by malicious UAVs requires advanced resources allocation and trajectory optimization strategies that align with the underlying communication mode.

RIS-enhanced Secure Communications RIS have emerged as a transformative technology for enhancing wireless communication performance [45–61]. By intelligently manipulating the propagation environment, RIS can significantly improve signal quality, reduce interference, and bolster system performance. However, the integration of RIS into UAV-enabled MEC systems for secure communications presents several unresolved issues. Effective deployment of RIS to maximize its potential in UAV-enabled MEC systems remains a critical issue. Whether RIS is carried by UAVs or deployed as static infrastructure, designing optimal placement and orientation strategies is essential. UAV-carried RIS, for instance, requires efficient trajectory planning to ensure both secure transmission and favorable channel conditions. Additionally, utilizing UAVs as relays in conjunction with RIS introduces additional complexity. Coordinating RIS reflection design with UAV relay operations to maximize secrecy rates and minimize latency is an open challenge. This necessitates joint optimization frameworks that integrate UAV trajectories, RIS configurations, and resource allocation strategies.

DRL-driven Adaptive Secure Communication Mechanisms DRL has demonstrated considerable potential in solving complex decision-making problems in dynamic environments. Its application to secure communications in UAV-enabled MEC systems is both promising and opening. On the one hand, in single-UAV scenarios, DRL can effectively handle dynamic trajectory planning and resource allocation to counteract malicious eavesdropping [62–78]. However, real-time adaptation to unpredictable eavesdropper behavior and environmental changes remains challenging. On the other hand, multi-UAV systems introduce additional complexity due to the need for coordination among UAVs. Designing DRL frameworks that enable collaborative strategies, such as cooperative jamming or distributed task allocation, is essential for enhancing security. By leveraging DRL, UAV-enabled MEC systems can dynamically adapt to evolving security threats, optimize operational efficiency, and ensure secure task execution. However, achieving this requires addressing challenges related to algorithm scalability and multi-agent collaboration.

1.5 Aim of the Brief

The aim of this brief is to provide a systematic exploration of secure communications in UAV-enabled MEC systems, introducing key challenges and identifying innovative solutions to enhance the security, efficiency, and adaptability of the systems. To this end, the open issues in terms of PLS-based secure communications for UAV-enabled MEC systems, RIS-enhanced secure communications, DRL-driven adaptive secure communication mechanisms and online real-time optimization strategies are introduced. The details will be presented in the following chapters. In Chap. 2, we study the research on PLS-based secure communications for UAV-enabled MEC systems, which involves TDMA-based and NOMA-based resource and trajectory optimization for secure communications. In Chap. 3, we explore RIS-based secure communications for UAV-enabled MEC systems, encompassing two scenarios: one where a UAV is equipped with a RIS to enhance computational support for devices, and another where a UAV functions as a relay node to facilitate secure and efficient computation. In Chap. 4, we present DRL-based secure communications for UAV-enabled MEC systems, where single UAV and multiple UAVs collaboration are considered. Finally, Chap. 5 gives the conclusion and potential future directions.

References

1. Q. Tang, F.R. Yu, R. Xie, A. Boukerche, T. Huang, Y. Liu, Internet of intelligence: a survey on the enabling technologies, applications, and challenges. IEEE Commun. Surv. Tutor. **24**(3), 1394–1434 (2022)
2. X. Wang, J. Mei, S. Cui, C.-X. Wang, X.S. Shen, Realizing 6G: the operational goals, enabling technologies of future networks, and value-oriented intelligent multi-dimensional multiple access. IEEE Netw. **37**(1), 10–17 (2023)
3. K.B. Letaief, Y. Shi, J. Lu, J. Lu, Edge artificial intelligence for 6G: vision, enabling technologies, and applications. IEEE J. Sel. Areas Commun. **40**(1), 5–36 (2022)
4. H. Li, K. Ota, M. Dong, Learning IoV in 6G: intelligent edge computing for internet of vehicles in 6G wireless communications. IEEE Wirel. Commun. **30**(6), 96–101 (2023)
5. M. Chafii, L. Bariah, S. Muhaidat, M. Debbah, Twelve scientific challenges for 6G: rethinking the foundations of communications theory. IEEE Commun. Surv. Tutor. **25**(2), 868–904 (2023)
6. X. Wang, Y. Han, V.C.M. Leung, D. Niyato, X. Yan, X. Chen, Convergence of edge computing and deep learning: a comprehensive survey. IEEE Commun. Surv. Tutor. **22**(2), 869–904 (2020)
7. M. Imran, M.N. Ali, M.S.U. Din, M.A.U. Rehman, B.-S. Kim, An efficient communication and computation resources sharing in information-centric 6G networks. IEEE Internet Things J. **11**(16), 27275–27294 (2024)
8. P. Porambage, J. Okwuibe, M. Liyanage, M. Ylianttila, T. Taleb, Survey on multi-access edge computing for internet of things realization. IEEE Commun. Surv. Tutor. **20**(4), 2961–2991 (2018)
9. N. Abbas, Y. Zhang, A. Taherkordi, T. Skeie, Mobile edge computing: a survey. IEEE Internet Things J. **5**(1), 450–465 (2018)
10. Y. Mao, C. You, J. Zhang, K. Huang, K.B. Letaief, A survey on mobile edge computing: the communication perspective. IEEE Commun. Surv. Tutor. **19**(4), 2322–2358 (2017)

11. P. Mach, Z. Becvar, Mobile edge computing: a survey on architecture and computation offloading. IEEE Commun. Surv. Tutor. **19**(3), 1628–1656 (2017)
12. K. Jiang, H. Zhou, X. Chen, H. Zhang, Mobile edge computing for ultra-reliable and low-latency communications. IEEE Commun. Stand. Mag. **5**(2), 68–75 (2021)
13. H. Zhou, Z. Zhang, Y. Wu, M. Dong, V.C.M. Leung, Energy efficient joint computation offloading and service caching for mobile edge computing: a deep reinforcement learning approach. IEEE Trans. Green Commun. Netw. **7**(2), 950–961 (2023)
14. T.X. Tran, A. Hajisami, P. Pandey, D. Pompili, Collaborative mobile edge computing in 5G networks: new paradigms, scenarios, and challenges. IEEE Commun. Mag. **55**(4), 54–61 (2017)
15. H. Liu, F. Eldarrat, H. Alqahtani, A. Reznik, X. de Foy, Y. Zhang, Mobile edge cloud system: architectures, challenges, and approaches. IEEE Syst. J. **12**(3), 2495–2508 (2018)
16. Y. Zeng, R. Zhang, T.J. Lim, Wireless communications with unmanned aerial vehicles: opportunities and challenges. IEEE Commun. Mag. **54**(5), 36–42 (2016)
17. N. Hossein Motlagh, T. Taleb, O. Arouk, Low-altitude unmanned aerial vehicles-based internet of things services: comprehensive survey and future perspectives. IEEE Internet Things J. **3**(6), 899–922 (2016)
18. A. Rucco, P.B. Sujit, A.P. Aguiar, J.B. de Sousa, F.L. Pereira, Optimal rendezvous trajectory for unmanned aerial-ground vehicles. IEEE Trans. Aerosp. Electron. Syst. **54**(2), 834–847 (2018)
19. C. Lin, G. Han, S.B.H. Shah, Y. Zou, L. Gou, Integrating mobile edge computing into unmanned aerial vehicle networks: an sdn-enabled architecture. IEEE Internet Things Mag. **4**(4), 18–23 (2021)
20. Y. Gao, X. Yuan, D. Yang, Y. Hu, Y. Cao, A. Schmeink, UAV-assisted MEC system with mobile ground terminals: DRL-based joint terminal scheduling and UAV 3D trajectory design. IEEE Trans. Veh. Technol. **73**(7), 10164–10180 (2024)
21. W. Lu, Y. Ding, Y. Gao et al., Resource and trajectory optimization for secure communications in dual unmanned aerial vehicle mobile edge computing systems. IEEE Trans. Ind. Inform. **18**(4), 2704–2713 (2022)
22. M. Zhao, W. Li, L. Bao, J. Luo, Z. He, D. Liu, Fairness-aware task scheduling and resource allocation in UAV-enabled mobile edge computing networks. IEEE Trans. Green Commun. Netw. **5**(4), 2174–2187 (2021)
23. Y. Wang, J. Zhu, H. Huang, F. Xiao, Bi-objective ant colony optimization for trajectory planning and task offloading in UAV-assisted MEC systems. IEEE Trans. Mob. Comput. **23**(12), 12360–12377 (2024)
24. C. Wang, Z. Yuan, P. Zhou, Z. Xu, R. Li, D.O. Wu, The security and privacy of mobile-edge computing: an artificial intelligence perspective. IEEE Internet Things J. **10**(24), 22008–22032 (2023)
25. W. Lu, Y. Ding, Y. Gao et al., Secure NOMA-based UAV-MEC network towards a flying eavesdropper. IEEE Trans. Commun. **70**(5), 3364–3376 (2022)
26. Y. Xu, T. Zhang, D. Yang, Y. Liu, M. Tao, Joint resource and trajectory optimization for security in UAV-assisted MEC systems. IEEE Trans. Commun. **69**(1), 573–588 (2021)
27. T. Bai, J. Wang, Y. Ren, L. Hanzo, Energy-efficient computation offloading for secure UAV-edge-computing systems. IEEE Trans. Veh. Technol. **68**(6), 6074–6087 (2019)
28. Y. Zhou, C. Pan, P.L. Yeoh et al., Secure communications for UAV-enabled mobile edge computing systems. IEEE Trans. Commun. **68**(1), 376–388 (2020)
29. M. Vucnik, T. Solc, U. Gregorc et al., Continuous integration in wireless technology development. IEEE Commun. Mag. **56**(12), 74–81 (2018)
30. M.Z. Chowdhury, M. Shahjalal, S. Ahmed, Y.M. Jang, 6G wireless communication systems: applications, requirements, technologies, challenges, and research directions. IEEE Open J. Commun. Soc. **1**, 957–975 (2020)
31. C. Wang, P. Zhang, N. Kumar, L. Liu, T. Yang, GCWCN: 6G-based global coverage wireless communication network architecture. IEEE Netw. **37**(3), 218–223 (2023)

32. F. Lu, G. Liu, W. Lu, Y. Gao, J. Cao, N. Zhao, A. Nallanathan, Resource and trajectory optimization for UAV-relay-assisted secure maritime MEC. IEEE Trans. Commun. **72**(3), 1641–1652 (2024)
33. Y. Zhang, Z. Kuang, Y. Feng, F. Hou, Task offloading and trajectory optimization for secure communications in dynamic user multi-UAV MEC systems. IEEE Trans. Mob. Comput. **23**(12), 14427–14440 (2024)
34. T. Zhao, F. Li, L. He, Secure video offloading in multi-UAV-enabled MEC networks: a deep reinforcement learning approach. IEEE Internet Things J. **11**(2), 2950–2963 (2024)
35. L. Zhong, Y. Liu, X. Deng, C. Wu, S. Liu, L.T. Yang, Distributed optimization of multi-role UAV functionality switching and trajectory for security task offloading in UAV-assisted MEC. IEEE Trans. Veh. Technol. **73**(12), 19432–19447 (2024)
36. X. Li, W. Huangfu, X. Xu, J. Huo, K. Long, Secure offloading with adversarial multi-agent reinforcement learning against intelligent eavesdroppers in UAV-enabled mobile edge computing. IEEE Trans. Mob. Comput. **23**(12), 13914–13928 (2024)
37. E.T. Michailidis, K. Maliatsos, D.N. Skoutas, D. Vouyioukas, C. Skianis, Secure UAV-aided mobile edge computing for IoT: a review. IEEE Access **10**, 86353–86383 (2022)
38. W. Mao, K. Xiong, Y. Lu, P. Fan, Z. Ding, Energy consumption minimization in secure multi-antenna UAV-assisted MEC networks with channel uncertainty. IEEE Trans. Wirel. Commun. **22**(11), 7185–7200 (2023)
39. J. Jung, S. Ahn, S. Kwon, S.-I. Park, J. Kang, Optimal UAV 3D trajectory design and resource allocation for secure mobile edge computing. IEEE Trans. Veh. Technol. https://doi.org/10.1109/TVT.2024.3500033
40. D. Kwon, S. Son, M. Kim, J. Lee, A. Kumar Das, Y. Park, A secure self-certified broadcast authentication protocol for intelligent transportation systems in UAV-assisted mobile edge computing environments. IEEE Trans. Intell. Transp. Syst. **25**(11), 19004–19017 (2024)
41. Y. He, K. Xiang, X. Cao, M. Guizani, Task scheduling and trajectory optimization based on fairness and communication security for multi-UAV-MEC system. IEEE Internet Things J. **11**(19), 30510–30523 (2024)
42. P. Chen, L. Luo, D. Guo, X. Luo, X. Li, Y. Sun, Secure task offloading for rural area surveillance based on UAV-UGV collaborations. IEEE Trans. Veh. Technol. **73**(1), 923–937 (2024)
43. P. Chen, X. Luo, D. Guo, Y. Sun, J. Xie, Y. Zhao, R. Zhou, Secure task offloading for MEC-aided-UAV system. IEEE Trans. Intell. Veh. **8**(5), 3444–3457 (2023)
44. A. Asheralieva, D. Niyato, Distributed dynamic resource management and pricing in the IoT systems with blockchain-as-a-service and UAV-enabled mobile edge computing. IEEE Internet Things J. **7**(3), 1974–1993 (2020)
45. H. Yang, S. Liu, L. Xiao, Y. Zhang, Z. Xiong, W. Zhuang, Learning-based reliable and secure transmission for UAV-RIS-assisted communication systems. IEEE Trans. Wirel. Commun. **23**(7), 6954–6967 (2024)
46. Y. Shang, Y. Peng, R. Ye, J. Lee, RIS-assisted secure UAV communication scheme against active jamming and passive eavesdropping. IEEE Trans. Intell. Transp. Syst. **25**(11), 16953–16963 (2024)
47. D. Diao, B. Wang, K. Cao, B. Zheng, J. Weng, J. Chen, Secure RIS deployment strategies for wireless-powered multi-UAV communication. IEEE Internet Things J. **11**(10), 18154–18166 (2024)
48. W. Wang, W. Ni, H. Tian, Y.C. Eldar, D. Niyato, UAV-mounted multi-functional RIS for combating eavesdropping in wireless networks. IEEE Wirel. Commun. Lett. **12**(10), 1667–1671 (2023)
49. R. Dong, B. Wang, K. Cao, J. Tian, T. Cheng, Secure transmission design of RIS enabled UAV communication networks exploiting deep reinforcement learning. IEEE Trans. Veh. Technol. **73**(6), 8404–8419 (2024)
50. L. Guo, J. Jia, J. Chen, X. Wang, Secure communication optimization in NOMA systems with UAV-mounted STAR-RIS. IEEE Trans. Inf. Forensics Secur. **19**, 2300–2314 (2024)

51. D. Diao, B. Wang, K. Cao, B. Zheng, R. Dong, T. Cheng, J. Chen, Reflecting elements analysis for secure and energy-efficient UAV-RIS system with phase errors. IEEE Wirel. Commun. Lett. **13**(2), 293–297 (2024)
52. Y. Liu, C. Huang, G. Chen, R. Song, S. Song, P. Xiao, Deep learning empowered trajectory and passive beamforming design in UAV-RIS enabled secure cognitive non-terrestrial networks. IEEE Wirel. Commun. Lett. **13**(1), 188–192 (2024)
53. Z.U.A. Tariq, E. Baccour, A. Erbad, M. Hamdi, M. Guizani, RL-based adaptive UAV swarm formation and clustering for secure 6G wireless communications in dynamic dense environments. IEEE Access **12**, 125609–125628 (2024)
54. Y. Wen, G. Chen, S. Fang, M. Wen, S. Tomasin, M.D. Renzo, RIS-assisted UAV secure communications with artificial noise-aware trajectory design against multiple colluding curious users. IEEE Trans. Inf. Forensics Secur. **19**, 3064–3076 (2024)
55. Y. Ge, J. Fan, J. Zhang, Active reconfigurable intelligent surface enhanced secure and energy-efficient communication of jittering UAV. IEEE Internet Things J. **10**(24), 22386–22400 (2023)
56. X. Liu, Y. Yu, B. Peng, X.B. Zhai, Q. Zhu, V.C.M. Leung, RIS-UAV enabled worst-case downlink secrecy rate maximization for mobile vehicles. IEEE Trans. Veh. Technol. **72**(5), 6129–6141 (2023)
57. S. Li, B. Duo, M.D. Renzo, M. Tao, X. Yuan, Robust secure UAV communications with the aid of reconfigurable intelligent surfaces. IEEE Trans. Wirel. Commun. **20**(10), 6402–6417 (2021)
58. R. Narmeen, A. Almadhor, A. Alkhayyat, P.-H. Ho, Secure beamforming for unmanned aerial vehicles equipped reconfigurable intelligent surfaces. IEEE Internet Things Mag. **7**(2), 30–37 (2024)
59. U.A. Mughal, Y. Alkhrijah, A. Almadhor, C. Yuen, Deep learning for secure UAV-assisted RIS communication networks. IEEE Internet Things Mag. **7**(2), 38–44 (2024)
60. X. Tang, T. Jiang, J. Liu, B. Li, D. Zhai, F. Yu, Z. Han, Secure communication with UAV-enabled aerial RIS: learning trajectory with reflection optimization. IEEE Trans. Intell. Veh. https://doi.org/10.1109/TIV.2023.3323973
61. Z.U.A. Tariq, E. Baccour, A. Erbad, M. Hamdi, Reinforcement learning for resilient aerial-IRS assisted wireless communications networks in the presence of multiple jammers. IEEE Open J. Commun. Soc. **5**, 15–37 (2024)
62. C. Liu, Y. Zhong, R. Wu, S. Ren, S. Du, B. Guo, Deep reinforcement learning based 3D-trajectory design and task offloading in UAV-enabled MEC system. IEEE Trans. Veh. Technol. **74**(2), 3185–3195 (2025)
63. M.N. Tariq, J. Wang, S. Raza, M. Siraj, M. Altamimi, S. Memon, Toward Optimal resource allocation: a multi-agent DRL based task offloading approach in multi-UAV-assisted MEC networks. IEEE Access **12**, 81428–81440 (2024)
64. C. Gu, F. Li, D. Liu, Y. Wu, H. Wang, DRL-based joint task scheduling and trajectory planning method for UAV-assisted MEC scenarios. IEEE Access **12**, 156224–156234 (2024)
65. T. Khurshid, W. Ahmed, M. Rehan, R. Ahmad, M.M. Alam, A. Radwan, A DRL strategy for optimal resource allocation along with 3D trajectory dynamics in UAV-MEC network. IEEE Access **11**, 54664–54678 (2023)
66. P.S. Aung, L.X. Nguyen, Y.K. Tun, Z. Han, C.S. Hong, Aerial STAR-RIS empowered MEC: a DRL approach for energy minimization. IEEE Wirel. Commun. Lett. **13**(5), 1409–1413 (2024)
67. B. Li, R. Yang, L. Liu, J. Wang, N. Zhang, M. Dong, Robust computation offloading and trajectory optimization for multi-UAV-assisted MEC: a multiagent DRL approach. IEEE Internet Things J. **11**(3), 4775–4786 (2024)
68. H. Wang, H. Zhang, X. Liu, K. Long, A. Nallanathan, Joint UAV placement optimization, resource allocation, and computation offloading for THz band: a DRL approach. IEEE Trans. Wirel. Commun. **22**(7), 4890–4900 (2023)
69. L. Dong, F. Jiang, M. Wang, Y. Peng, X. Li, Deep progressive reinforcement learning-based flexible resource scheduling framework for IRS and UAV-assisted MEC system. IEEE Trans. Neural Netw. Learn. Syst. **36**(2), 2314–2326 (2025)
70. W. Lee, T. Kim, Multiagent reinforcement learning in controlling offloading ratio and trajectory for multi-UAV mobile-edge computing. IEEE Internet Things J. **11**(2), 3417–3429 (2024)

71. T. Du, X. Gui, X. Teng, K. Zhang, D. Ren, Dynamic trajectory design and bandwidth adjustment for energy-efficient UAV-assisted relaying with deep reinforcement learning in MEC IoT system. IEEE Internet Things J. **11**(23), 37463–37479 (2024)
72. A. Gao, S. Zhang, Q. Zhang, Y. Hu, S. Liu, W. Liang, S. Ng, Task offloading and energy optimization in hybrid UAV-assisted mobile edge computing systems. IEEE Trans. Veh. Technol. **73**(8), 12052–12066 (2024)
73. Y. Liu, J. Yan, X. Zhao, Deep reinforcement learning based latency minimization for mobile edge computing with virtualization in maritime UAV communication network. IEEE Trans. Veh. Technol. **71**(4), 4225–4236 (2022)
74. T. Liu, T. Zhang, J. Loo, Y. Wang, Deep reinforcement learning-based resource allocation for UAV-enabled federated edge learning. J. Commun. Inf. Netw. **8**(1), 1–12 (2023)
75. T. Deng, Y. Wang, J. Li, R. Cao, Y. Gu, J. Hu, X. Tang, M. Huang, W. Liu, S. Li, Entropy normalization SAC-based task offloading for UAV-assisted mobile-edge computing. IEEE Internet Things J. **11**(15), 26220–26233 (2024)
76. S. Goudarzi, S. Ahmad Soleymani, M. Hossein Anisi, A. Jindal, P. Xiao, Optimizing UAV-assisted vehicular edge computing with age of information: an SAC-based solution. IEEE Internet Things J. **12**(5), 4555–4569 (2025)
77. A.M. Seid, G.O. Boateng, S. Anokye, T. Kwantwi, G. Sun, G. Liu, Collaborative computation offloading and resource allocation in multi-UAV-assisted IoT networks: a deep reinforcement learning approach. IEEE Internet Things J. **8**(15), 12203–12218 (2021)
78. Z. Ning, Y. Yang, X. Wang, Q. Song, L. Guo, A. Jamalipour, Multi-agent deep reinforcement learning based UAV trajectory optimization for differentiated services. IEEE Trans. Mob. Comput. **23**(5), 5818–5834 (2024)

Chapter 2
PLS-Based Secure Communications for UAV-Enabled MEC Systems

With the rapid advancement of wireless communication technologies, the emergence of intelligent applications, such as facial recognition, smart grids, autonomous driving, and interactive gaming, has driven an exponential increase in data traffic. These applications are often characterized by computationally intensive tasks, imposing higher demands on the processing capabilities of devices. Moreover, the IoE era has raised expectations for broader communication network coverage to ensure ubiquitous high-performance services. Mobile cloud computing enables terminal devices to offload computational tasks to cloud servers and thereby mitigating their resource limitations. However, mobile cloud computing relies heavily on backhaul links for data transmission, which not only consumes significant link resources but also introduces additional latency. These limitations make it challenging to meet the stringent requirements of next-generation networks for high computational performance.

As a flexible and efficient technology, UAV-enabled MEC enables rapid deployment, enhances the quality of communication links, and alleviates network congestion, providing effective offloading services for ground terminal devices. However, in UAV-enabled MEC systems with multiple coexisting devices, signal interference among devices can significantly degrade transmission quality.

To address this issue, TDMA transmission divides time into multiple independent, non-overlapping slots, allocating each slot exclusively to a specific device, thereby effectively avoiding signal interference. Furthermore, NOMA, a key technology in future wireless communications, utilizes advanced SIC techniques for signal decoding. This not only enhances signal reception performance but also reduces the reliance on channel state information feedback, saving channel bandwidth and energy consumption. Additionally, NOMA allows multiple devices to share the same link resources, significantly improving resource utilization.

However, during the process of task data offloading in practical communication scenarios, malicious eavesdroppers may intercept confidential information, posing significant risks to the security of data transmission. PLS techniques leverage the

W. Lu et al., *Secure Communications in Unmanned Aerial Vehicle-Enabled Mobile Edge Computing Systems*, SpringerBriefs in Computer Science,
https://doi.org/10.1007/978-981-96-9611-6_2

inherent characteristics of communication channels and transmission methods to provide robust data transmission security for UAV-enabled MEC systems. Notably, existing studies predominantly focus on countering threats posed by ground-based eavesdroppers while overlooking the potential risk of UAVs serving as aerial eavesdropping devices.

In this chapter, we consider two secure communication schemes for the UAV-enabled MEC system under TDMA and NOMA transmission. In the system, UAV Server (UAV_S) assists GUs in offloading tasks. In order to reduce UAV Eavesdropper's eavesdropping on offloading information, GJ sends interference signals. We aim to improve the secure communication performance of the system by optimizing the UAV_S trajectory and wireless resources with the guarantee of the basic secure computing requirements of each GU. The main contributions of this chapter are summarized as follows.

- First, a secure communication scheme integrating TDMA protocol with coordinated resource-trajectory optimization is presented. The mathematical formulation aims to maximize the worst-case secure computation capacity of GUs through multidimensional optimization involving temporal resource partitioning, power allocation strategies, local computation scheduling, and continuous UAV trajectory design. Key constraints encompass UAV flight speed, UAV anti collision, energy ability, local calculation ability and UAV_S CPU frequency. Real-world applicability is ensured by incorporating GUs' heterogeneous computational task profiles. Given the NP-hard non-convex nature of the original problem, we implement a decomposition methodology utilizing SCA for convex relaxation and BCD for variable subset alternation, achieving suboptimal solutions through sequential parameter updating.
- Then, to enhance resource utilization efficiency, this study develops a secure communication framework by integrating NOMA technology with joint resource allocation and trajectory optimization. An optimization model is established to maximize the average secure computational capacity through coordinated management of multiple parameters: channel correlation coefficients between UAV_S and ground users, CPU processing frequency, transmission power allocation, local computation resources, and UAV_S flight trajectory. Addressing the challenges posed by unknown UAV_E locations, binary decision variables, multivariate coupling effects, and inherent non-convex properties, the proposed approach implements worst-case security analysis through rigorous mathematical derivations to mitigate positioning uncertainty. Leveraging SCA techniques with BCD methodology and alternating optimization principles, we derive an efficient solution strategy for this multidimensional optimization problem, achieving superior performance in secure computational throughput.
- Finally, the simulation results reveal that when compared against benchmark approaches, both developed schemes exhibit superior effectiveness in strengthening the secure communication capabilities within the considered UAV-enabled MEC framework.

The subsequent sections of this chapter are structured as follows: Sect. 2.1 provides the related studies. Section 2.2 elaborates on the TDMA-based resource and trajectory optimization, validating the effectiveness of the proposed scheme through comprehensive analyses that encompass the system model, problem formulation, solution development, experimental results, and corresponding evaluations. Section 2.3 focuses on the NOMA-based resource and trajectory optimization, similarly demonstrating the superiority of the proposed approach by addressing the system model, problem formulation, solution methodology, experimental findings, and detailed analysis.

2.1 Related Studies

As a technology that effectively reduces network congestion while optimizing computational performance, MEC plays a critical role in multiple 5G application ecosystems [1]. Pham et al. demonstrated that partitioning the backhaul bandwidth and assigning computational resources to MEC networks could effectively minimize system processing costs while enhancing computational performance [2]. Leveraging their high mobility and cost-effectiveness, UAVs offer rapid deployment capabilities to establish efficient emergency support systems and auxiliary infrastructure for IoT implementation in remote geographical areas [3, 4]. Mozaffari et al. devised a systematic methodology to maximize user-centric bit transmission efficiency via intelligent UAV coverage area optimization, operating under fairness-guaranteed resource management schemes and UAV flight time restrictions [4]. The deployment of MEC-enabled UAVs further enables dynamic wireless link optimization and robust processing offloading services for ground terminals [5–12]. Specifically, Yu et al. demonstrated that deploying UAVs as aerial base stations (BSs) effectively addresses shadow fading and signal congestion issues in terrestrial coverage regions between conventional IoT devices and ground-based BSs [5]. Zhou et al. studied a framework designed to optimize computational performance in UAV-MEC systems while addressing energy consumption and mobility limitations [6]. Du et al. proposed a UAV-MEC framework employing TDMA protocol to enhance system efficiency through coordinated optimization of UAV deployment and computational resource allocation [7]. Wang et al. studied a dual-layer optimization framework to enhance service delivery for dense mobile ground users through strategic deployment of multiple UAVs and coordinated system resource allocation [8]. Liu et al. evaluated the joint resource allocation and collaborative offloading optimization framework under ground station requirements and channel state variations within UAV-assisted MEC system architectures [9]. Hu et al. proposed a useful strategy to obtain the optimized solution of the UAV-MEC system [10]. Zhang et al. developed an optimization framework for multi-UAV MEC networks to enhance computational processing efficiency through coordinated resource allocation across aerial platforms [11]. Liu et al. proposed a decentralized two-phase resource allocation strategy to address energy-efficient and secure task offloading challenges in air-to-ground MEC networks [12].

Meanwhile, NOMA significantly enhances spectral efficiency and data transmission rates [13–16]. Capitalizing on these benefits, UAV-assisted MEC networks extensively adopt NOMA to enable scalable computation offloading services for massive GUs [17–23]. Cui et al. implemented a mode to utilize OMA and NOMA in BS-UAV communication links to optimize network throughput [17]. Na et al. developed a cluster-NOMA-based cooperative optimization algorithm that mitigates inter-channel interference while boosting uplink capacity [18]. Li et al. pointed out that NOMA-MEC integration effectively alleviates computational offloading and caching bottlenecks for data-intensive applications [19]. Nevertheless, wireless task delegation remains vulnerable to eavesdropping by malicious nodes, introducing critical security vulnerabilities in UAV-MEC systems.

PLS technology enables robust secure communication through intelligent exploitation of wireless channel characteristics and adaptive transmission methods [24–33]. Rupasinghe et al. investigated a scheme to improve UAV network security via protected zone spatial configurations [24]. Mu et al. maximized security efficiency through coordinated deployment of computing and jamming UAVs [25]. Sheng et al. improved the security throughput of the worst users by allocating the time slots to send confidential information or artificial noise [28]. Cao et al. proposed an anti-eavesdropping scheme through beamforming in NOMA networks [29]. Sun et al. showed that the UAV communication performed by NOMA not only expands the coverage but also improves the security [30]. Duo et al. proposed a security optimization strategy in the presence of mobile eavesdroppers to ensure that the confidential information between UAV and GUs is not leaked [31]. Xu et al. studied the security optimization scheme in UAV-MEC system to prevent eavesdroppers from stealing useful offloading information [32]. Li et al. studied the rate improving design in case of imperfect eavesdropping channels [33].

2.2 TDMA-Based Resource and Trajectory Optimization for Secure Communications

2.2.1 System Model for TDMA-Based Secure Communications

As depicted in Fig. 2.1, we consider a UAV-enabled MEC system for secure communications with TDMA transmission. The system consists of two UAVs named UAV_S and UAV_E, a GJ and K GUs. UAV_S functions as a server, assisting GUs in completing computational tasks, and UAV_E operates as a mobile eavesdropper, attempting to intercept the offloaded information from GUs to UAV_S along its flight trajectory. To mitigate the eavesdropping risk, the GJ transmits interference signals that obscure the offloaded information. Since UAV_S has prior knowledge of the interference signal generated by the GJ, it can effectively cancel

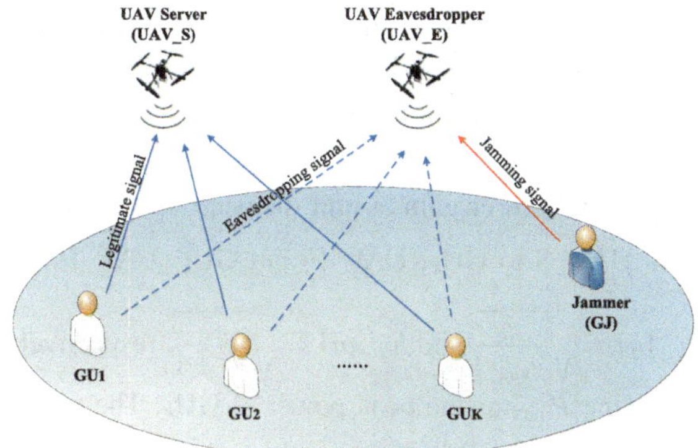

Fig. 2.1 A UAV-enabled MEC system for secure communications with TDMA transmission

this interference from the received signal. In contrast, UAV_E, being unaware of the GJ's presence, treats all received signals as useful, thereby experiencing the interference as noise. We assume UAV_S, UAV_E, GUs and GJ are each equipped with a single antenna.

The horizontal coordinates of GU_k $(k = 1, \ldots, K)$ and GJ are defined as $w_k = (x_k, y_k)^T$, $w_j = (x_j, y_j)^T$, respectively. It is assumed that the UAVs have prior knowledge of each GU's location and the CSI for all links within the UAV-enabled MEC secure communication system through synthetic aperture radar or other means [32]. This information enables precise estimation of the upper bound of the secure communication computation capacity. Let the UAV flight duration be denoted by $T, T \geq 0$. The position of UAV_i $(i \in \{S, E\})$ at any time t is expressed as $q_i(t), t \in [0, T]$. Both UAVs are assumed to operate at fixed altitudes H_i to perform their designated tasks. For simplicity, the period T is divided into N equal time slots, with each slot having a duration of $\delta_t = T/N$. Accordingly, the horizontal position of UAV_i in the time slot n is expressed as $q_i[n] = (x_i[n], y_i[n])^T$.

Suppose UAV_i flies from the given start position q_i^I to the end position q_i^F during the flight period. The trajectory of UAV_E is predetermined, and the trajectory of UAV_S is subject to optimization based on the system's configuration. Define the maximum speed of UAV_S as $V_s^{\max}$. Consequently, the maximum allowable displacement of UAV_S in a time slot $l_s^{\max}$ should satisfy $l_s^{\max} = V_s^{\max}\delta_t$. The movement constraint of UAV_S can be expressed as

$$q_s[1] = q_s^I, q_s[N] = q_s^F, \tag{2.1a}$$

$$||q_s[n+1] - q_s[n]|| \leq l_s^{\max}, \forall n = 1, 2, ..., N-1. \tag{2.1b}$$

To ensure collision avoidance between UAV_S and UAV_E, a minimum separation distance $d_{\min}$ is defined. Then, we have

$$||q_s[n] - q_e[n]||^2 \geq d_{\min}^2, \forall n \in \{1, 2..., N\}. \tag{2.2}$$

In the time slot n, the distance between UAV_S and GU$_k$, UAV_E and GU$_k$, UAV_E and GJ are $d_{k,s}[n] = \sqrt{H_s^2 + ||q_s[n] - w_k||^2}$, $d_{k,e}[n] = \sqrt{H_e^2 + ||q_e[n] - w_k||^2}$ and $d_{j,e}[n] = \sqrt{H_e^2 + ||q_e[n] - w_j||^2}$, respectively.

The channels from UAVs to GUs are defined as the LoS channel. Define β_0 as the channel power gain at unit distance. In the time slot n, the channel coefficient from UAV_S to GU$_k$, UAV_E and GU$_k$, UAV_E and GJ are $h_{k,s}[n] = \sqrt{\frac{\beta_0}{d_{k,s}^2[n]}}$, $h_{k,e}[n] = \sqrt{\frac{\beta_0}{d_{k,e}^2[n]}}$ and $h_{j,e}[n] = \sqrt{\frac{\beta_0}{d_{j,e}^2[n]}}$, respectively.

Define $P_{\max}$ as the peak power of GU$_k$. The transmit power of GU$_k$ in the time slot n, $p_k[n]$, needs to satisfy

$$0 \leq p_k[n] \leq P_{\max}, \forall k, n. \tag{2.3}$$

2.2.2 *Problem Formulation for Secure Capacity Maximization*

The task offloading mechanism for GUs employs a TDMA framework, where each time slot n is further subdivided into K sub-slots. The time allocated to GU$_k$ is $\tau_k[n]\delta_t$ in each time slot n, where $\tau_k[n]$ represents the time allocation factor, which needs to satisfy

$$\sum_{k=1}^{K} \tau_k[n] \leq 1, 0 \leq \tau_k[n] \leq 1, \forall k, n. \tag{2.4}$$

2.2.2.1 Communication Model

Given the prior knowledge of GJ's transmitted signals possessed by UAV_S, UAV_S is able to separate the interference signal from the signals it receives. Therefore, in each time slot n the SINR of UAV_S receiving GU$_k$ signals is $r_{k,s}[n] = \frac{|h_{k,s}[n]|^2 p_k[n]}{\delta_s^2}$. Conversely, UAV_E lacks capability to discriminate between legitimate GU$_k$ signals and GJ's interference. Thus, the SINR of the signal received by UAV_E in the time slot n is $r_{k,e}[n] = \frac{|h_{k,e}[n]|^2 p_k[n]}{|h_{j,e}[n]|^2 P_j + \delta_e^2}$, where P_j as the GJ's transmit power, δ_s^2 and δ_e^2 represents the AWGN at UAV_S and UAV_E, respectively.

Therefore, the task offloading rate from GU$_k$ to UAV_S is formulated as

$$R_{k,s}[n] = \tau_k[n]\log_2\left(1 + \frac{|h_{k,s}[n]|^2 p_k[n]}{\delta_s^2}\right), \forall k, n. \tag{2.5}$$

The eavesdropping rate for transmissions from GU$_k$ to UAV_E is formulated as

$$R_{k,e}[n] = \tau_k[n]\log_2\left(1 + \frac{|h_{k,e}[n]|^2 p_k[n]}{|h_{j,e}[n]|^2 P_j + \delta_e^2}\right), \forall k, n. \tag{2.6}$$

Consequently, the secure computation offloading rate from GU$_k$ to UAV_S is formulated as

$$R_{k,\text{sec}}[n] = \left(R_{k,\text{s}}[n] - R_{k,e}[n]\right)^+, \forall k, n. \tag{2.7}$$

2.2.2.2 Computing Model

GUs adopt a hybrid computation strategy, executing a portion of tasks locally while offloading the remaining portion to UAV_S for processing. Let c_k denote the CPU cycles required for GU$_k$ to calculate per bit of data, $l_{\text{loc},k}[n]$ represent the local calculation bits of GU$_k$ in the time slot n, and $F_k^{\max}$ specify the peak CPU frequency of GU$_k$. Subject to the device's maximum computational capability, the local processing at GU$_k$ must comply with

$$c_k l_{\text{loc},k}[n] \leq \delta_t F_k^{\max}, \forall k, n. \tag{2.8}$$

Define c_s as the CPU cycles required for UAV_S to calculate per bit of data, $F_s^{\max}$ as the maximum CPU frequency of UAV_S, respectively. Similarly, the number of secure calculation bits of GU$_k$ at UAV_S cannot exceed the calculation capacity of UAV_S. Therefore, GU$_k$ calculation offloading tasks needs to satisfy

$$c_s B \delta_t R_{k,\text{sec}}[n] \leq \delta_t \tau_k[n] F_s^{\max}, \forall k, n. \tag{2.9}$$

where B represents the bandwidth.

Let Q_m denote the minimum secure computational requirement per user in each time slot n. To ensure compliance with fundamental computational demands across all users, we derive

$$l_{\text{loc},k}[n] + B\tau_k[n]\delta_t R_{k,\text{sec}}[n] \geq Q_m, \forall k, n. \tag{2.10}$$

The energy consumed when GU$_k$ calculates locally in the time slot n is $l_{\text{loc},k}[n] = \frac{k_k (c_k l_{\text{loc},k}[n])^3}{\delta_t^2}$, where k_k represents GU$_k$'s effective capacitance coefficient.

The energy consumed by GU$_k$ in the process of transmitting the signal can be expressed as $\tau_k[n]\delta_t p_k[n]$. The energy consumption constraint of GU$_k$ in the whole period T is

$$\frac{1}{T}\sum_{n=1}^{N}\left(\frac{k_k (c_k l_{\text{loc},k}[n])^3}{\delta_t^2} + \tau_k[n]\delta_t p_k[n]\right) \leq P_{\text{ave}}^k, \forall k, n. \tag{2.11}$$

where P_{ave}^k is the average transmission power of GU_k. The total energy consumed by GU_k in each time is divided into two parts, one part is used for the energy consumed when GUs is locally calculated, and the other part is used for the energy consumed when GUs transmit information to UAV_S. The constraint (2.11) indicates that the power consumed on average should not be larger than P_{ave}^k.

2.2.2.3 Problem Formulation

In the given period T, GU_k's the secure calculation capacity is defined as the average number of secure calculation bits of GU_k that can be reached, as follows,

$$\overline{R}_{k,\text{sec}} = \frac{1}{T}\left(B\delta_t \sum_{n=1}^{N} \tau_k[n] R_{k,\text{sec}}[n] + \sum_{n=1}^{N} l_{\text{loc},k}[n]\right), \forall k, n. \tag{2.12}$$

Our target is to maximize the minimum secure calculation capacity, thereby improving the security of the system, which is formulated as

$$\begin{aligned}
&(\text{P1}): \max_{\{\tau_k[n], p_k[n], l_{\text{loc},k}[n], q_s[n]\}} \min_{\forall k} \overline{R}_{k,\text{sec}} \\
&s.t. \quad (2.1), (2.2), (2.3), (2.4), (2.8), (2.9), (2.10), (2.11).
\end{aligned}$$

Due to the non-convexity of constraints (2.2), (2.9), (2.10) and (2.11), problem (P1) is multi-variable coupled and non-convex, which is hard to be solved.

2.2.3 Problem Solution

To solve the problem (P1), we introduce auxiliary variables s, $s_{1,k}[n]$, $s_{2,k}[n]$. Then, the optimized variables are $Z = \{\tau_k[n], p_k[n], l_{\text{loc},k}[n], q_s[n], s_{1,k}[n], s_{2,k}[n]\}$, the optimization problem (P1) is equivalently transformed as

$$(\text{P2}): \max_{Z} s \tag{2.13a}$$

$$s.t. \quad (2.1), (2.2), (2.3), (2.4), (2.8), (2.11).$$

$$s \le \frac{1}{T}\left(B\delta_t \sum_{n=1}^{N} \tau_k[n](s_{1,k}[n] - s_{2,k}[n]) + \sum_{n=1}^{N} l_{\text{loc},k}[n]\right), \forall k, n \tag{2.13b}$$

$$s_{1,k}[n] \le \log_2\left(1 + \frac{|h_{k,s}[n]|^2 p_k[n]}{\delta_s^2}\right), \forall k, n \tag{2.13c}$$

$$s_{2,k}[n] \geq \log_2\left(1 + \frac{|h_{k,e}[n]|^2 p_k[n]}{|h_{j,e}[n]|^2 P_j + \delta_e^2}\right), \forall k, n \tag{2.13d}$$

$$c_s B\left(s_{1,k}[n] - s_{2,k}[n]\right) \leq F_s^{\max}, \forall k, n \tag{2.13e}$$

$$l_{\text{loc},k}[n] + B\tau_k[n]\delta_t\left(s_{1,k}[n] - s_{2,k}[n]\right) \geq Q_m, \forall k, n. \tag{2.13f}$$

Since the target is to maximize the minimum secure calculation capacity $\overline{R}_{k,\text{sec}}$, the lower bound of $\overline{R}_{k,\text{sec}}$ can be represented by the auxiliary variable s, which can be represented by (2.13a). The operator $[\cdot]^+$ in (2.7) can be omitted, because we can set $p_k[n] = 0, l_{\text{loc},k}[n] = 0$ to obtain the value of 0 at least. The lower bound of the task offloading rate from GU$_k$ to UAV_S $R_{k,s}[n]$ is expressed by $\tau_k[n]s_{1,k}[n]$, and the upper bound of the eavesdropping rate from GU$_k$ to UAV_E $R_{k,e}[n]$ is expressed by $\tau_k[n]s_{2,k}[n]$, as shown in (2.13c) and (2.13d), respectively. In (2.13b), the equation has to be hold, or the value of s approaches infinity. $R_{k,\text{sec}}[n]$ can be expressed by $\tau_k[n](s_{1,k}[n] - s_{2,k}[n])$. Thus constraint (2.9) and (2.10) can be replaced as (2.13e) and (2.13f), respectively.

The problem (P2) is solved by decomposing with the following two steps. Step 1, optimize the variables $Z\backslash q_s[n]$ with given trajectory $\{q_s[n]\}$. Step 2, optimize trajectory $\{q_s[n]\}$ with given $Z\backslash q_s[n]$.

2.2.3.1 Step 1: Optimizing $Z\backslash q_s[n]$ with Given $q_s[n]$

For the given trajectory $\{q_s[n]\}$, the problem (P2) is re-expressed as

$$\begin{aligned} (\text{P3}): &\max_{Z\backslash\{q_s[n]\}} \ s \\ s.t.\quad &(2.3), (2.4), (2.8), (2.11), (2.13\text{b})\text{–}(2.13\text{f}). \end{aligned}$$

Although the problem (P3) is still non-convex because the non-convexity of the constraints (2.11), (2.13b), (2.13c), (2.13d) and (2.13f). We can solve it through SCA technique, which can approximately solve non-convex optimal problems, in which time allocation $A = \{\tau_k[n]\}$, GU$_k$'s transmission power allocation $B = \{p_k[n]\}$, and GU$_k$'s local calculation allocation $C = \{l_{\text{loc},k}[n]\}$ can be obtained in an alternating manner by considering the others as given.

Time Allocation

For the given GU$_k$'s transmit power allocation B and GU$_k$'s local calculation allocation C, the optimization problem is formulated as

$$\begin{aligned} (\text{P3.1}): &\max_{\{A\},\{s_{1,k}[n],s_{2,k}[n]\}} \ s \\ s.t.\quad &(2.4), (2.11), (2.13\text{b})\text{–}(2.13\text{f}). \end{aligned} \tag{2.14a}$$

Note that (P3.1) is typically convex as the constraints are linear, which can be solved by standard optimization techniques, e.g., CVX.

Transmit Power Allocation

For the given time allocation A and GU_k's local calculation allocation C, the optimization problem is formulated as

$$\begin{aligned}(\mathrm{P3.2}):\quad &\max_{\{B\},\{s_{1,k}[n],s_{2,k}[n]\}} \quad s\\ &s.t.\quad (2.3), (2.11), (2.13b)\text{–}(2.13f).\end{aligned}$$

Since the non-convexity of the constraints (2.13c) and (2.13d), the optimization problem (P3.2) is non-convex, which is hard to obtain the optimal solution. The optimization problem (P3.2) can be solved through applying SCA technique, in which (P3.2) is approximated to a convex problem in each iteration. Then, transmission power allocation of GU_k can be obtained by updating it iteratively.

Assuming that $\{p_k^r[n]\}$ denotes as the transmit power of GU_k after the r_{th} iteration. Convex function can be a first-order Taylor expansion of the global lower bound, thus we convert approximately (2.13c) as

$$s_{1,k}[n] \le \log_2\left(1+\frac{|h_{k,s}[n]|^2 p_k^r[n]}{\delta_s^2}\right)+\frac{1}{\ln 2}\frac{|h_{k,s}[n]|^2}{\delta_s^2}\frac{\left(p_k[n]-p_k^r[n]\right)}{\left(1+\frac{|h_{k,s}[n]|^2 p_k^r[n]}{\delta_s^2}\right)}, \forall k,n. \tag{2.15}$$

Similarly for (2.13d) we have

$$\begin{aligned}s_{2,k}[n] \ge &\log_2\left(1+\frac{|h_{k,e}[n]|^2 p_k^r[n]}{|h_{j,e}[n]|^2 P_j+\delta_e^2}\right)+\frac{1}{\ln 2}\frac{|h_{k,e}[n]|^2}{|h_{j,e}[n]|^2 P_j+\delta_e^2}*\\ &\frac{\left(p_k[n]-p_k^r[n]\right)\left(|h_{j,e}[n]|^2 P_j+\delta_e^2\right)}{\left(|h_{j,e}[n]|^2 P_j+\delta_e^2+|h_{k,e}[n]|^2 p_k^r[n]\right)}, \forall k,n.\end{aligned} \tag{2.16}$$

Thus (P3.2) is reformulated as

$$\begin{aligned}(\mathrm{P3.2.1}):\quad &\max_{\{B\},\{s_{1,k}[n],s_{2,k}[n]\}} \quad s\\ &s.t.\quad (2.3), (2.11), (2.13b), (2.13e), (2.13f), (2.15), (2.16).\end{aligned}$$

Note that (P3.2.1) is a convex problem. We can solve it through standard optimization techniques.

Local Calculation Allocation
For the given time allocation A and GU$_k$'s transmit power allocation B, the optimization problem is formulated as

$$\text{(P3.3)}: \max_{\{C\},\{s_{1,k}[n],s_{2,k}[n]\}} s$$
$$s.t. \quad (2.8), (2.11), (2.13b)\text{–}(2.13f).$$

Since the constraints of (P3.3) are linear, thus (P3.3) is convex. We can solve it by standard optimization techniques.

Thus, the optimization solution of (P3) can be obtained by alternately solving problems (P3.1), (P3.2) and (P3.3).

2.2.3.2 Step 2: Optimizing $q_s[n]$ with Given $Z\backslash q_s[n]$

For the given time allocation A, GU$_k$'s transmit power allocation B and GU$_k$'s local calculation allocation C, the problem (P2) is re-expressed as

$$\text{(P4)}: \max_{\{q_s[n]\},\{s_{1,k}[n],s_{2,k}[n]\}} s$$
$$s.t. \quad (2.1), (2.2), (2.13b)\text{–}(2.13f).$$

Since the non-convexity of (2.2) and (2.13c), the problem (P4) is non-convex, which is hard to be solved. It can be solved through SCA technique, in which (P4) is approximated to a convex problem in each iteration. Then we can obtain trajectory optimization of UAV_S by updating it iteratively.

Assume that $\{q_s^r[n]\}$ represents the trajectory of UAV_S after the r_{th} iteration, thus for (2.2) we have

$$||q_s^r[n] - q_e[n]||^2 + 2||q_s^r[n] - q_e[n]||||q_s[n] - q_s^r[n]|| \geq d_{\min}^2, \forall n \in \{1, 2, ..., N\}. \tag{2.17}$$

For (2.13c), it can be transformed into

$$\begin{aligned} s_{1,k}[n] \leq &\log_2((H_s^2 + ||q_s[n] - w_k||^2)\delta_s^2 + \beta_0 p_k[n]) \\ &- \log_2((H_s^2 + ||q_s[n] - w_k||^2)\delta_s^2), \forall k, n. \end{aligned} \tag{2.18}$$

With SCA technique, the right side in (2.18) can be expressed by the lower-bounded $B_{1,k}[n] - B_{2,k}[n]$ approximately, in which $B_{1,k}[n]$ and $B_{2,k}[n]$ denote as

$$B_{1,k}[n] = \log_2((H_s^2 + ||q_s^r[n] - w_k||^2)\delta_s^2 + \beta_0 p_k[n]) \\ + \frac{1}{\ln 2} \frac{2(||q_s^r[n] - w_k||)\delta_s^2(q_s[n] - q_s^r[n])}{((H_s^2 + ||q_s^r[n] - w_k||^2)\delta_s^2 + \beta_0 p_k[n])}, \forall k, n. \tag{2.19}$$

$$B_{2,k}[n] = \log_2((H_s^2 + ||q_s^r[n] - w_k||^2)\delta_s^2) \\ + \frac{2}{\ln 2} \frac{(||q_s^r[n] - w_k||)\delta_s^2(q_s[n] - q_s^r[n])}{(H_s^2 + ||q_s^r[n] - w_k||^2)\delta_s^2}, \forall k, n. \tag{2.20}$$

Constraint (2.18) is rewritten as

$$s_{1,k}[n] \leq B_{1,k}[n] - B_{2,k}[n], \forall k, n. \tag{2.21}$$

Thus, (P4) can be converted to

$$\text{(P4.1)}: \max_{\{q_s[n]\}, \{s_{1,k}[n], s_{2,k}[n]\}} \quad s$$
$$s.t. \quad (2.1), (2.13b), (2.13d), (2.13e), (2.17), (2.21).$$

(P4.1) is a convex problem, thus we can solve it through standard optimization techniques efficiently.

In conclusion, we can solve problems (P3) and (P4) in an alternative manner to ensure that the objective function of the optimizing problem (P1) is monotonically non-decreasing with all variables updating.

2.2.4 Simulation Results

In this section, simulation results are presented to validate the effectiveness of our proposed scheme. In the proposed scheme, 5 GUs are distributed randomly in the area of $400 \times 400\,\text{m}^2$. The location of GJ is fixed at $[0, 0]^T$. UAV_S needs to fly from $q_s^I = [-200, -10]^T$ to $q_s^F = [200, -10]^T$, and UAV_E flies from $q_e^I = [-200, 50]^T$ to $q_e^F = [200, -60]^T$ with fixed speed. The maximum flying speed of UAV_i is $V_i^{\max} = 50\,\text{m/s}$, the minimum distance between UAV_S and UAV_E to avoid collision is $d_{\min} = 1\,\text{m}$.

Figure 2.2 shows the convergence performance of the proposed scheme with different values of $P_{\max}$ and T. In Fig. 2.2, we can find that our proposed scheme will be converged with different values of $P_{\max}$ and T and the system's performance becomes better with larger $P_{\max}$ and T.

Figure 2.3 shows the optimized trajectory for UAV_S and the given flight trajectory for UAV_E of our proposed scheme with different T. In order to clearly reflect the trajectories of UAV_S and UAV_E, the corresponding positions of UAV_S and UAV_E in each time slot n are marked with different marks. It can

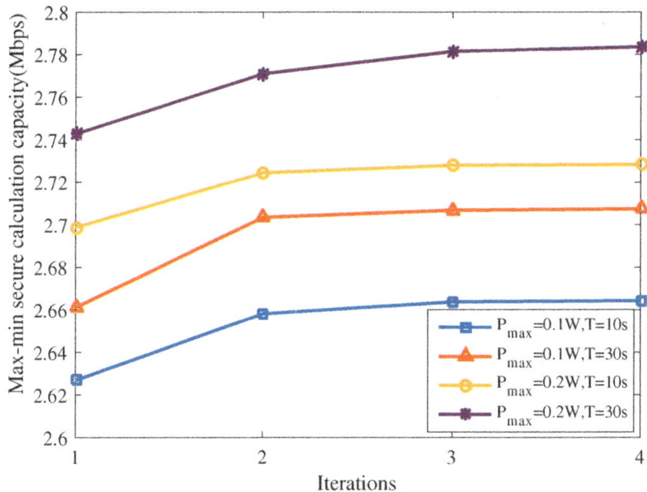

Fig. 2.2 Convergence performance of proposed scheme with different $P_{\max}$ and T

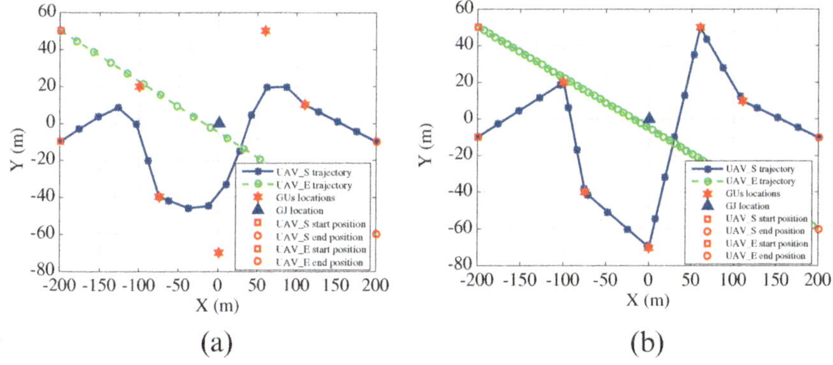

Fig. 2.3 Optimized trajectory for UAV_S and UAV_E with different T. (**a**) $T = 10\,\text{s}$, $P_{\max} = 0.1\,\text{W}$. (**b**) $T = 30\,\text{s}$, $P_{\max} = 0.1\,\text{W}$

be seen that UAV_S tends to be closer to GUs to receive the offloading information during the flight. In the case of a short time $T = 10\,\text{s}$, as shown in Fig. 2.3a, UAV_S flies as close as possible to each GUs. When T is sufficient large, e.g., $T = 30\,\text{s}$, as shown in Fig. 2.3b, UAV_S flies to hover directly above the GUs, thereby enhancing secure calculation capacity.

Figure 2.4 shows the optimized speed for UAV_S and UAV_E of our proposed scheme with different T in each time slot. In Fig. 2.4, V_S and V_E represent the speed of UAV_S and UAV_E, respectively. UAV_E flies from the start position to the end position with a constant speed. Note that the total flight distance of UAV_E is same in Fig. 2.4a, b, but T is different, thus the speed of UAV_E is different. The trajectory of UAV_S needs to be optimized to maximize the secure calculation

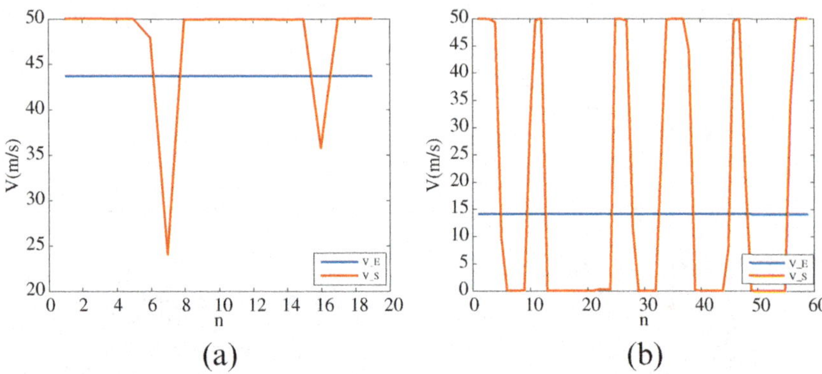

Fig. 2.4 Optimized speed for UAV_S and UAV_E with different T. (**a**) $T = 10\,\text{s}$, $P_{\max} = 0.1\,\text{W}$. (**b**) $T = 30\,\text{s}$, $P_{\max} = 0.1\,\text{W}$

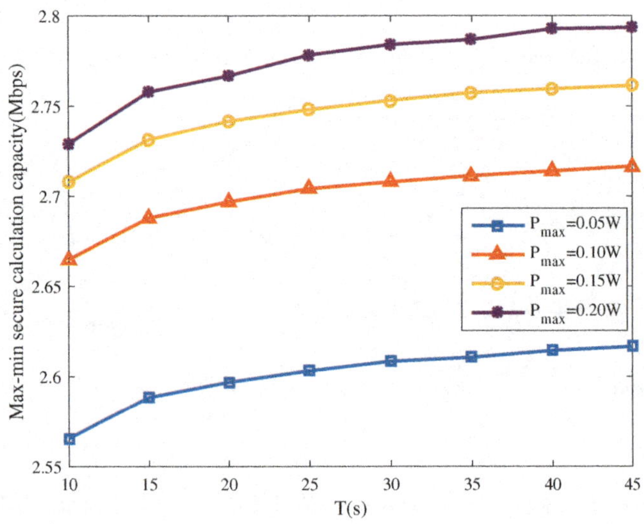

Fig. 2.5 The secure calculation capacity versus T

capacity. Thus, it will tend to hover as close as possible to the GUs for better information offloading, and the speed will change accordingly. When $T = 10\,\text{s}$, as shown in Fig. 2.4a, UAV_S flies nearly with its maximum speed to the end position due to the limited fly time. However, when $T = 30\,\text{s}$, as shown in Fig. 2.4b, with sufficient time, UAV_S approaches the GUs at its maximum speed, then hovered directly above the GUs where the offloading task from the GUs was received in the best condition.

Figure 2.5 shows the max-min secure calculation capacity, which reflects the secure communication performance of Dual-UAV-MEC system, versus flight time T with different peak power of GUs $P_{\max}$. In Fig. 2.5, we can find that the max-

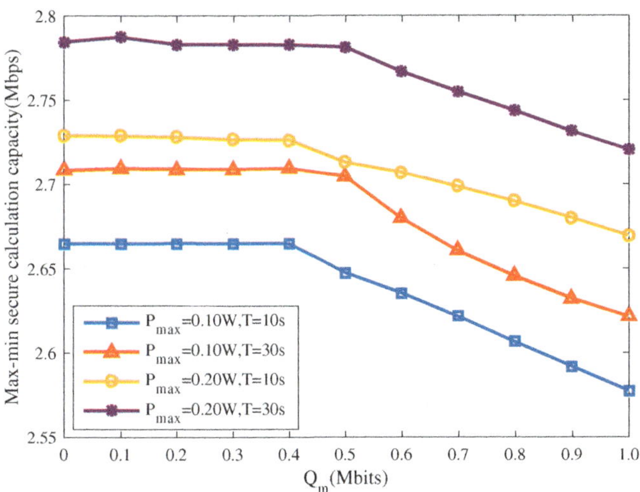

Fig. 2.6 The secure calculation capacity versus Q_m

min secure calculation capacity becomes larger when T increases. It is because that UAV_S is able to gain more time to hover in the best position to receive the offloading information when T is larger. We can also observe from Fig. 2.5 that with the increase of $P_{\max}$, the max-min secure calculation capacity will becomes larger. It is because that when $P_{\max}$ is larger, GUs can have more energy to send more offloading information.

To reflect the effect of required computing bits Q_m on the system performance, Fig. 2.6 shows the max-min secure calculation capacity versus Q_m with different peak power of GUs $P_{\max}$. In Fig. 2.6, we find that when Q_m is with small value, e.g., smaller than 0.5 Mbits, the max-min secure calculation capacity decrease slowly. It is because that the maximum CPU frequency of each GU is set to be 1 GHz, which can guarantee the maximum number of tasks calculated locally. However, when Q_m further increases, as GU$_k$ has limited computing power, more tasks have to be offloaded to UAV_S for calculation, which gives UAV_E more opportunities to eavesdrop on the information sent by GU$_k$ to UAV_S. Thus, the performance will be worse as Q_m increases.

Figure 2.7 shows the effectiveness of our proposed scheme, in which the performance comparison is made with four benchmark schemes. In Scheme 1, UAV_S flies with straight line from $[-200, -10]^T$ to $[200, -10]^T$, and the power and local calculation is optimized with our proposed method while the time is equally allocated. In Scheme 2, UAV_S flies with straight line from $[-200, -10]^T$ to $[200, -10]^T$, and the time and local calculation is optimized with our proposed method while the power is fixed to 0.05 W. In Scheme 3, UAV_S flies with straight line from $[-200, -10]^T$ to $[200, -10]^T$, and the power, time and local calculation is optimized with our proposed method. In Scheme 4, UAV_S location, users' transmit power, jamming power and offloading ratio are jointly optimized to maximize the

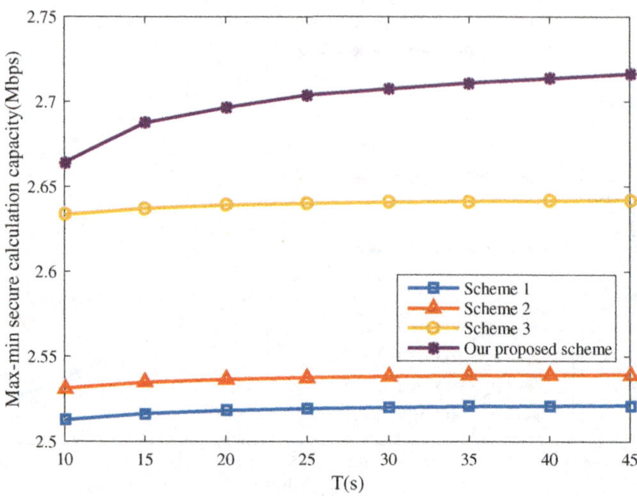

Fig. 2.7 The secure calculation capacity comparison with the varying T

minimum secrecy capacity. Compared with Scheme 1, Scheme 2 and Scheme 3 versus flight time T. We do not compare with Scheme 4 since the position of UAVs are fixed in Scheme 4, the secure calculation capacity is not related to flight time T.

2.2.5 *Summary*

In this section, we proposed a secure communication scheme for the UAV-enabled MEC system, in which UAV_S assists to calculate the offloading tasks of GUs. To reduce the eavesdropping of offloading information by UAV_E, GJ sends interference signals. Through optimizing resources and trajectory of UAV_S, we aim to maximize GUs minimum secure calculation capacity with the constraints of UAV flight speed, UAV anti collision, GUs transmit power, GUs local calculation ability, UAV_S CPU frequency and GUs computing task requirements. Due to the non-convexity of the problem, we combine SCA and BCD algorithms to solve the optimization problem. The simulation results show that compared with the benchmark schemes, the scheme we proposed can improve the system's secure calculation capacity.

2.3 NOMA-Based Resource and Trajectory Optimization for Secure Communications

2.3.1 System Model for NOMA-Based Secure Communications

Figure 2.8 shows the proposed UAV-enabled MEC system for secure communications with NOMA transmission, in which the legitimate UAV_S carries the MEC server to serve K GUs, denoted by $\mathcal{K} = \{1, 2, ..., K\}$. UAV_S computes offloaded information of tasks from GUs, while the potential mobile UAV_E eavesdrops the offloaded tasks information. In order to enhance the security performance of the system, a GJ is set on the ground to disturb UAV_E's eavesdropping by sending artificial jamming signals to disrupt the eavesdropping. We assume that UAV_S has prior knowledge of the jamming signal sent by GJ because UAV_S and GJ belong to the legitimate network, the jamming signal sent by GJ are friendly to UAV_S. Thus, UAV_S will not be affected by the artificial jamming signals. However, UAV_E is unaware of GJ's presence because UAV_E is a mobile eavesdropper and it does not belong to the legitimate network. It treats all signals eavesdropped during flight as GUs' signals. Thus, the jamming signal sent by GJ will interfere UAV_E. All of GJ, GUs and UAVs in the system have a single antenna.

We consider a three-dimensional Cartesian coordinate system [32], the coordinates of GJ and $\text{GU}_k, k \in \mathcal{K}$, are represented as $w_j = \left(x_j, y_j, 0\right)^T, w_k = (x_k, y_k, 0)^T$, respectively. Assuming UAV_S and UAV_E fly at a certain altitude of H_s and H_e, respectively. The total flight time of UAVs is denoted as T. The positions of UAV_S and UAV_E are denoted as $q_s(t) = (x_s(t), y_s(t), H_s)$, $q_e(t) =$

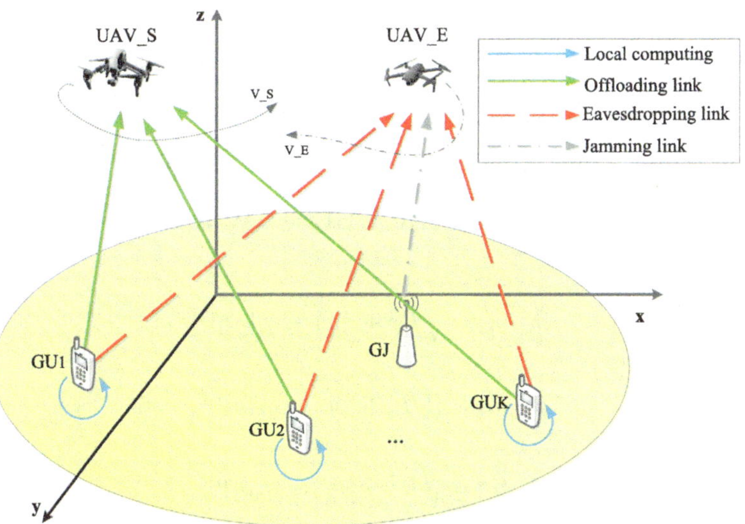

Fig. 2.8 A UAV-enabled MEC systems for secure communications with NOMA transmission

$(x_e(t), y_e(t), H_e), t \in [0, T]$, respectively. For convenience, we adopt discrete trajectory. The total flight time T is divided evenly into N time slots, e.g., $\delta_t = T/N$. The position UAV_S and UAV_E are denoted as $q_s[n] = (x_s[n], y_s[n], H_s)$, $q_e[n] = (x_e[n], y_e[n], H_e), n \in [1, 2, ..., N]$, respectively. The position of UAV_S is related to the origin of the three-dimensional Cartesian coordinate system. The position information can be get by GPS positioning or other methods. We assume that UAV_S has known the position of all GUs and GJ, and the channel state information of the corresponding links in advance by means of synthetic aperture radar, etc. We consider passive eavesdropping, in which UAV_E disguises itself as a normal UAV flying in the sky to hide itself, which makes it difficult for the legitimate network to accurately detect and track [33]. Thus, the position of UAV_E is imperfectly known at UAV_S. We consider a bounded eavesdropper location error model given by $||q_e[n] - \tilde{q}_e[n]|| \le r_e$, where $\tilde{q}_e[n]$ is the estimated position of UAV_E, r_e is the maximum estimation error of the position of UAV_E. In practice, the maximum estimation error of the position of UAV_E will not exceed the distance between UAV_E and GU, i.e., $r_e \le ||\tilde{q}_e[n] - w_k||$. Denote q_s^I and q_s^F as UAV_S flight start point and end point, respectively. Denote q_e^I and q_e^F as UAV_E flight start point and end point, respectively. UAV_S flies from q_s^I to q_s^F within T to assist computing offloading. UAV_E flies from q_e^I to q_e^F within T to carry out its eavesdropping flight mission. Denote UAV_S maximum flight speed as $V_s^{\max}$. Then, UAV_S trajectory should satisfy

$$||q_s[n+1] - q_s[n]|| \le V_s^{\max}\delta_t, \forall n = 1, 2, ..., N-1, \tag{2.22}$$

$$q_s[1] = q_s^I, \tag{2.23}$$

$$q_s[N] = q_s^F. \tag{2.24}$$

Define the minimum secure distance between UAVs to avoid collision as $d_{\min}$, which needs to satisfy

$$d_{\min}^2 \le ||q_s[n] - q_e[n]||^2, \forall n = 1, 2, ..., N. \tag{2.25}$$

The distance between GU_k and UAV_S, GJ and UAV_E, GU_k and UAV_E in slot n are denoted as

$$d_{k,s}[n] = \sqrt{H_s^2 + ||w_k - q_s[n]||^2}, \tag{2.26}$$

$$d_{j,e}[n] = \sqrt{H_e^2 + ||w_j - q_e[n]||^2}, \tag{2.27}$$

$$d_{k,e}[n] = \sqrt{H_e^2 + ||w_k - q_e[n]||^2}. \tag{2.28}$$

Thus, the channel gain between GU$_k$ and UAV_S, GJ and UAV_E, GU$_k$ and UAV_E in slot n are denoted as

$$h_{k,s}[n] = \sqrt{\frac{\beta_0}{d_{k,s}^2[n]}}, \tag{2.29}$$

$$h_{j,e}[n] = \sqrt{\frac{\beta_0}{d_{j,e}^2[n]}}, \tag{2.30}$$

$$h_{k,e}[n] = \sqrt{\frac{\beta_0}{d_{k,e}^2[n]}}, \tag{2.31}$$

where β_0 represents the path loss at the reference distance of $d = 1$ m.

Define $p_k[n]$ as the transmit power of GU$_k$, which is not larger than the peak power of GU$_k$,

$$0 \le p_k[n] \le P_{\max}, \forall k, n. \tag{2.32}$$

2.3.2 Problem Formulation for Secure Capacity Maximization

GUs utilize NOMA transmission for information offloading, in which GUs can simultaneously access to UAV_S by sharing the same time and bandwidth. UAV_S performs SIC to decode signals in descending order of channel gain, i.e., the signals of GUs far from UAV_S with lower channel gains are regarded as the interference to those signals that are closer to UAV_S with higher channel gains.

Assume that binary variable $\lambda_{k,l}[n]$ is used to represent the varying channel relationship coefficient between the channel of GU$_k$ and UAV_S and the channel of GU$_l$ and UAV_S in slot n. Since the unit channel power gain is the same, we use the relationship between the distance of GU$_k$ and UAV_S and the distance of GU$_l$ and UAV_S to denote $\lambda_{k,l}[n]$, which can be written as

$$\lambda_{k,l}[n] = \begin{cases} 1, if \ d_{k,s}[n] \le d_{l,s}[n], \\ 0, if \ d_{k,s}[n] > d_{l,s}[n], \end{cases} \tag{2.33a}$$

$$\lambda_{k,l}[n] \in \{0, 1\}, \tag{2.33b}$$

$$\lambda_{k,l}[n] + \lambda_{l,k}[n] = 1, \forall k, l, n, \tag{2.33c}$$

where $d_{l,s}[n]$ represents the distance between UAV_S and GU$_l$ in slot n. As can be seen from (2.33a), if $d_{k,s}[n] \le d_{l,s}[n]$, we have $h_{k,s}[n] \ge h_{l,s}[n]$. Thus, $\lambda_{k,l}[n] = 1$, which denotes that the channel condition of GU$_k$ is better than GU$_l$ and the task information of GU$_l$ interferes with GU$_k$, otherwise $\lambda_{k,l}[n] = 0$. In order to avoid the interference in the SIC decoding process, we have (2.33b) to restrain it, which indicates that when the signal of GU_l interferes with the signal offloading of GU_k, the signal of GU_k will no longer interfere with the signal offloading of GU_l due to the SIC decoding.

2.3.2.1 Communication Model

As mentioned above, UAV_E is unaware of GJ's presence. Therefore, the jamming signals sent by GJ incurs a random effect on UAV_E. UAV_S has prior knowledge of the jamming signal sent by GJ. It will not be affected by the artificially disturbed signals. Thus, the signal-to-interference-plus-noise-ratio received at UAV_S and UAV_E are denoted as

$$r_{k,s}[n] = \frac{|h_{k,s}[n]|^2 p_k[n]}{\sum\limits_{l \neq \mathcal{K}, l \in \kappa} \lambda_{k,l}[n]|h_{l,s}[n]|^2 p_l[n] + \delta_s^2}, \forall k, n, \tag{2.34}$$

$$r_{k,e}[n] = \frac{|h_{k,e}[n]|^2 p_k[n]}{|h_{j,e}[n]|^2 P_j + \sum\limits_{z \in K_k} |h_{z,e}[n]|^2 p_z[n] + \delta_e^2}, \forall k, n, \tag{2.35}$$

where $h_{z,e}[n]$ is channel gain between GU_z and UAV_E, $K_k = \{z | z \in \kappa, |h_{z,e}| \leq |h_{k,e}|\}$ denotes the group of GUs whose channel gain to UAV_E is worse than that of GU_k to UAV_E, P_j denotes GJ transmit power, δ_s^2 and δ_e^2 denote power of Gaussian noise received at the UAV_S and the UAV_E, respectively.

Therefore, the achievable information offloading rate from UAV_S to GU_k and the achievable information eavesdropping rate from UAV_E to GU_k are denoted as

$$R_{k,s}[n] = \log_2 \left(1 + r_{k,s}[n]\right), \tag{2.36}$$

$$R_{k,e}[n] = \log_2 \left(1 + r_{k,e}[n]\right). \tag{2.37}$$

The security information offloading rate can be obtained as

$$R_{k,\mathrm{sec}}[n] = \left(R_{k,s}[n] - R_{k,e}[n]\right)^+, \forall k, n. \tag{2.38}$$

2.3.2.2 Computation Model

GU_k adopts partial offloading computation strategy, in which some tasks information of GU_k are calculated locally, and the remaining information tasks are offloaded to UAV_S for computation. Denote $l_{\mathrm{loc},k}[n]$ as the number of bits GU_k computes locally in slot n. Denote c_s and c_k as the required CPU computation cycles for computing a bit of information at UAV_S and GU_k, respectively. Denote $F_s^{\max}$

and $F_k^{\max}$ as UAV_S and GU$_k$ maximum CPU frequency, respectively. Since GU$_k$ cannot compute more than its maximum local computation capacity, it should satisfy

$$c_k l_{\text{loc},k}[n] \leq F_k^{\max} \delta_t, \forall k, n. \tag{2.39}$$

Denote $f_k[n]$ as the CPU computation frequency allocated to GU$_k$ at UAV_S to compute the offloaded information of tasks, which needs to satisfy

$$\sum_{k=1}^{K} f_k[n] \leq F_s^{\max}, \forall n, \tag{2.40a}$$

$$0 \leq f_k[n] \leq F_s^{\max}, \forall k, n. \tag{2.40b}$$

Similarly, the number of security computation bits offloaded from GU$_k$ to UAV_S are limited to the computation capacity allocated by UAV_S to GU$_k$. Thus, the security offloading computation from GU$_k$ to UAV_S has the following constraints

$$c_s B R_{k,\text{sec}}[n]\delta_t \leq f_k[n]\delta_t, \forall k, n, \tag{2.41}$$

where B denotes channel bandwidth.

To guarantee the minimum security computation requirements for all the GUs, the amount of GU$_k$ local computation and offloading computation assisted by UAV_S should be larger than the minimum security computation requirement, it should satisfy

$$l_{\text{loc},k}[n] + B\delta_t R_{k,\text{sec}}[n] \geq Q_m, \forall k, n, \tag{2.42}$$

where Q_m denotes the minimum security computation requirements for GUs.

Denote k_k as the effective capacitance coefficient of GU$_k$. Then, the energy consumption of GU$_k$ in local computation can be written as $\frac{k_k \left(c_k l_{\text{loc},k}[n]\right)^3}{\delta_t^2}$.

The energy consumption of GU$_k$ in computing the information of tasks locally and transmitting offloading task information to UAV_S over time T cannot be larger than the average energy budget of GU$_k$, it should satisfy

$$\sum_{n=1}^{N} \left(p_k[n]\delta_t + \frac{k_k \left(c_k l_{\text{loc},k}[n]\right)^3}{\delta_t^2} \right) \leq P_{\text{ave}}^k T, \forall k, n, \tag{2.43}$$

where P_{ave}^k denotes GU$_k$ average power budget.

The average security computation capacity of the NOMA-based UAV-MEC system in time T is obtained as

$$\overline{R}_{\text{sec}} = \frac{1}{KT} \sum_{k=1}^{K} \left(\sum_{n=1}^{N} l_{\text{loc},k}[n] + B \sum_{n=1}^{N} R_{k,\text{sec}}[n] \delta_t \right), \tag{2.44}$$

which denotes the average of the total security computation capacity in all the time slots.

2.3.2.3 Problem Formulation

To maximize the average security computation capacity of the system, with respect to varying channel relationship coefficient $\lambda_{k,l}[n]$, transmit power $p_k[n]$, CPU computation frequency $f_k[n]$, local computation $l_{\text{loc},k}[n]$ and UAV_S trajectory $q_s[n]$ are optimized, the optimization problem is formulated as

$$\text{(P1)}: \max_{\{\lambda_{k,l}[n], f_k[n], p_k[n], l_{\text{loc},k}[n], q_s[n]\}} \overline{R}_{\text{sec}} \tag{2.45}$$

$$s.t. \quad (2.22), (2.23), (2.24), (2.25), (2.32), (2.33), (2.39), (2.40), (2.41), (2.42), (2.43).$$

2.3.3 Problem Solution

To simplify the original problem (P1), we introduce auxiliary variables $\hat{s}$, $\hat{s}_{1,k}[n]$, $\hat{s}_{2,k}[n]$. Then, the original problem (P1) can be equivalently rewritten as

$$\text{(P1.1)}: \max_{\hat{z}} \hat{s} \tag{2.46a}$$

$$s.t. \quad (2.22), (2.23), (2.24), (2.25), (2.32), (2.33), (2.39), (2.40), (2.43)$$

$$KT\hat{s} \le \sum_{k=1}^{K} \sum_{n=1}^{N} \left(l_{\text{loc},k}[n] + B\delta_t \left(\hat{s}_{1,k}[n] - \hat{s}_{2,k}[n] \right) \right), \forall n, \tag{2.46b}$$

$$\hat{s}_{1,k}[n] \le R_{k,s}[n], \forall k, n, \tag{2.46c}$$

$$\hat{s}_{2,k}[n] \ge R_{k,e}[n], \forall k, n, \tag{2.46d}$$

$$c_k B \left(\hat{s}_{1,k}[n] - \hat{s}_{2,k}[n] \right) \le f_k[n], \forall k, n, \tag{2.46e}$$

$$B\delta_t \left(\hat{s}_{1,k}[n] - \hat{s}_{2,k}[n] \right) + l_{\text{loc},k}[n] \ge Q_m, \forall k, n, \tag{2.46f}$$

where $\hat{z} = \{\lambda_{k,l}[n], f_k[n], p_k[n], l_{\text{loc},k}[n], q_s[n], \hat{s}_{1,k}[n], \hat{s}_{2,k}[n]\}$. $\hat{s}$ represents the lower bound of the average security computation capacity $\overline{R}_{\text{sec}}$, and $\hat{s}_{1,k}[n]$ represents the lower bound of the instantaneous tasks information offloading rate $R_{k,s}[n]$, which can be represented by (2.46b) and (2.46c). $\hat{s}_{2,k}[n]$ represents the upper bound of the instantaneous tasks information eavesdropping rate $R_{k,e}[n]$, which can be represented by (2.46d). $\hat{s}$ needs to satisfy the equality constraint in (2.46b), otherwise its value will tend to infinity. Thus, the optimization target can be represented by (2.46a). Constraints (2.41) and (2.42) are rewritten as (2.46e) and (2.46f), respectively.

Due to the uncertainty of UAV_E position, $R_{k,e}[n]$ in the objective function is implicit. In order to facilitate the derivation, we maximize the average security computation capacity of all GUs in the worst case. In Lemma 2.1, we obtain the upper bound of $R_{k,e}[n]$ and approximate it to the achievable information eavesdropping rate from UAV_E to GU$_k$.

Lemma 2.1 *The upper bound of $R_{k,e}[n]$ is expressed as*

$$\begin{aligned} l R_{k,e}^{ub}[n] =& \log_2\left(1 + r_{k,e}^{ub}[n]\right) \\ =& \log_2\left(1 + \frac{p_k[n]|\hat{h}_{k,e}[n]|^2}{|\hat{h}_{j,e}[n]|^2 P_j + \sum\limits_{z=1, z\in K_k} p_z[n]|\hat{h}_{z,e}[n]|^2 + \delta_e^2}\right), \end{aligned} \tag{2.47}$$

where

$$|\hat{h}_{k,e}[n]|^2 = \frac{\beta_0}{H_e^2 + (||q_e[n] - w_k|| - r_e)^2}, \tag{2.48}$$

$$|\hat{h}_{z,e}[n]|^2 = \frac{\beta_0}{H_e^2 + (||q_e[n] - w_z|| + r_e)^2}, \tag{2.49}$$

$$|\hat{h}_{j,e}[n]|^2 = \frac{\beta_0}{H_e^2 + \left(||q_e[n] - w_j|| + r_e\right)^2}, \tag{2.50}$$

indicate the maximum estimation value of $|h_{k,e}[n]|^2$, the minimum estimation value of $|h_{z,e}[n]|^2$ and the minimum estimation value of $|h_{j,e}[n]|^2$.

Proof According to the maximum estimate error previously proposed, $||q_e[n] - \tilde{q}_e[n]|| \le r_e$, we can apply triangle inequality and anti-triangle inequality to solve the uncertainty of UAV_E position, as follows,

$$\begin{aligned} l||q_e[n] - w_k|| \ge& ||q_e[n] - w_k|| - ||q_e[n] - \tilde{q}_e[n]|| \\ \ge& ||q_e[n] - w_k|| - r_e, \end{aligned} \tag{2.51a}$$

$$\begin{aligned} l||q_e[n]-w_z|| &\le ||q_e[n]-w_z|| + ||q_e[n]-\tilde{q}_e[n]|| \\ &\le ||q_e[n]-w_z|| + r_e, \end{aligned} \tag{2.51b}$$

$$\begin{aligned} l||q_e[n]-w_j|| &\le ||q_e[n]-w_j|| + ||q_e[n]-\tilde{q}_e[n]|| \\ &\le ||q_e[n]-w_j|| + r_e. \end{aligned} \tag{2.51c}$$

Thus, the upper bound of $R_{k,e}[n]$ is expressed as (2.47). □

Due to the multi-variables coupling constraints and binary constraints, problem (P1.1) is non-convex. We solve (P1.1) by optimizing the block structure of the variables in two steps. In Step 1, we optimize the block of variables $\{\hat{z}\backslash q_s[n]\}$ with fixed UAV_S trajectory $\{q_s[n]\}$. In Step 2, we optimize UAV_S trajectory $\{q_s[n]\}$ with fixed $\{\hat{z}\backslash q_s[n]\}$.

2.3.3.1 Resource Allocation

With fixed UAV_S trajectory $q_s[n]$, problem (P1.1) is reformulated as

$$\begin{aligned} &(\text{P2}):\ \max_{\hat{z}\backslash\{q_s[n]\}}\ \hat{s} \\ &s.t.\quad (2.32), (2.33), (2.39), (2.40), (2.43), (2.46\text{b})\text{–}(2.46\text{f}). \end{aligned} \tag{2.52}$$

Problem (P2) is difficult to obtain the solution for two reasons. First, constraint (2.39) is a binary constraint, which is not continuous. Second, constraint (2.46c) and (2.46d) are both non-convex.

We use SCA and BCD technique to solve (P2), in which varying channel relationship coefficient optimization $A = \lambda_{k,l}[n]$, transmit power allocation $B = p_k[n]$, CPU computation frequency allocation $C = f_k[n]$ and local computation allocation $D = l_{\text{loc},k}[n]$ can be obtained by updating in an iterative way by considering the others fixed.

Varying Channel Relationship Coefficient Optimization

For fixed transmit power allocation B, CPU computation frequency allocation C and local computation allocation D, we formulate the varying channel relationship coefficient optimization problem as

$$\begin{aligned} &(\text{P2.1}):\ \max_{\{A\},\{\hat{s}_{1,k}[n],\hat{s}_{2,k}[n]\}}\ \hat{s} \\ &s.t.\quad (2.33), (2.46\text{b})\text{–}(2.46\text{f}). \end{aligned} \tag{2.53}$$

Introducing $\tilde{\lambda}_{k,l}[n]$ into binary constraint (2.33), it can be equivalently converted as

$$\lambda_{k,l}[n] = \tilde{\lambda}_{k,l}[n], \forall k, l, n, \tag{2.54a}$$

$$\lambda_{k,l}[n]\left(1 - \tilde{\lambda}_{k,l}[n]\right) = 0, \tag{2.54b}$$

$$\lambda_{k,l}[n]d_{k,s}[n] \leq d_{l,s}[n], \forall k, n. \tag{2.54c}$$

It can be seen that (2.54a) and (2.54b) are exactly equivalent to (2.33b) and (2.33c). From (2.54c), if $d_{l,s}[n] > d_{k,s}[n]$, $\lambda_{k,l}[n]$ could be 1 or 0, and if $d_{l,s}[n] < d_{k,s}[n]$, we have $\lambda_{k,l}[n] = 0$. However, $\lambda_{k,l}[n]$ and $\lambda_{l,k}[n]$ are constrained by (2.33c), if $\lambda_{k,l}[n]$ or $\lambda_{l,k}[n]$ is 1, the other one must be 0, then (2.54c) is equivalent to (2.33a). Thus, $\tilde{\lambda}_{k,l}[n]$ can effectively solve the binary constraint of (P2.1).

Then, problem (P2.1) is converted as

$$\text{(P2.1.1)}: \max_{\{A,\tilde{\lambda}_{k,l}[n]\},\{\hat{s}_{1,k}[n],\hat{s}_{2,k}[n]\}} \hat{s} \tag{2.55}$$

$$s.t. \quad \text{(2.46b)–(2.46f), (2.54).}$$

Problem (P2.1.1) can be solved by standard optimization techniques, e.g., CVX.

Transmit Power Allocation

For fixed varying channel relationship coefficient optimization A, CPU computation frequency allocation C and local computation allocation D, we formulate the transmit power allocation problem (P2.2) as

$$\text{(P2.2)}: \max_{\{B\},\{\hat{s}_{1,k}[n],\hat{s}_{2,k}[n]\}} \hat{s} \tag{2.56}$$

$$s.t. \quad \text{(2.32), (2.43), (2.46b)–(2.46f).}$$

Note that problem (P2.2) is non-convex due to the non-convexity of (2.46c) and (2.46d), which is hard to solve. We can apply SCA technique to approximate the problem (P2.2) as a convex problem in each iteration, which can obtain the transmit power allocation solution by updating it iteratively.

Substituting (2.34) into (2.36) and (2.46c), we can obtain

$$\hat{s}_{1,k}[n] \leq F_{1,k}[n] - \log_2\left(\sum_{l\neq k, l\in\mathcal{K}} \lambda_{k,l}[n]p_l[n]|h_{l,s}[n]|^2 + \delta_s^2\right), \forall k, n, \tag{2.57}$$

where $F_{1,k}[n] = \log_2\left(\sum_{l\neq k, l\in\mathcal{K}} \lambda_{k,l}[n]p_l[n]|h_{l,s}[n]|^2 + p_k[n]|h_{k,s}[n]|^2 + \delta_s^2\right)$.

Note that the convex function can be obtained by the global lower bound with the first-order Taylor expansion. In Lemma 2.2, the lower bound of $\hat{s}_{1,k}[n]$ is approximately obtained.

Lemma 2.2 *Equation (2.57) is approximately transformed as*

$$ll\hat{s}_{1,k}[n] \leq F_{1,k}[n] - \log_2\left(\sum_{l\neq k, l\in\mathcal{K}} \lambda_{k,l}[n]|h_{l,s}[n]|^2 p_l^r[n] + \delta_s^2\right) - \frac{1}{\ln 2}\frac{\sum_{l\neq k, l\in\mathcal{K}} \lambda_{k,l}[n]|h_{l,s}[n]|^2\left(p_l[n] - p_l^r[n]\right)}{\sum_{l\neq k, l\in\mathcal{K}} \lambda_{k,l}[n]|h_{l,s}[n]|^2 p_l^r[n] + \delta_s^2}, \forall k, n, \tag{2.58}$$

where $p_l^r[n]$ denotes the transmit power acquired by GU_l *in r_{th} iteration.*

Similarly, substituting (2.35) into (2.37) and (2.46d), (2.46d) is equivalent as

$$\hat{s}_{2,k}[n] \geq F_{2,k}[n] + \log_2\left(\sum_{z\in K_k} |h_{z,e}[n]|^2 p_z[n] + A_1[n] + |h_{k,e}[n]|^2 p_k[n]\right), \forall k, n. \tag{2.59}$$

where $F_{2,k}[n] = -\log_2\left(|h_{j,e}[n]|^2 P_j + \sum_{z\in K_k} |h_{z,e}[n]|^2 p_z[n] + \delta_e^2\right)$ and $A_1[n] = |h_{j,e}[n]|^2 P_j + \delta_e^2$.

Then, (2.59) can be approximately transformed as

$$1\hat{s}_{2,k}[n] \geq F_{2,k}[n] + \log_2\left(\sum_{z\in K_k} |h_{z,e}[n]|^2 p_z^r[n] + A_1[n] + |h_{k,e}[n]|^2 p_k^r[n]\right) + \frac{\sum_{z\in K_k} |h_{z,e}[n]|^2\left(p_z[n] - p_z^r[n]\right) + |h_{k,e}[n]|^2\left(p_k[n] - p_k^r[n]\right)}{\ln 2 \sum_{z\in K_k} |h_{z,e}[n]|^2 p_z^r[n] + A_1[n] + |h_{k,e}[n]|^2 p_k^r[n]}. \tag{2.60}$$

where $p_z^r[n]$ and $p_k^r[n]$ represent the transmit power acquired by GU_z and GU_k in r_{th} iteration, respectively.

Thus, the problem (P2.2) is transformed as

$$(\mathrm{P2.2.1}): \max_{\{B\},\{\hat{s}_{1,k}[n],\hat{s}_{2,k}[n]\}} \hat{s} \tag{2.61}$$

$$s.t. \quad (2.32), (2.43), (2.46b), (2.46e), (2.46f), (2.58).(2.60).$$

Problem (P2.2.1) is a typical convex problem since all of its constraints are convex, e.g., constraint (2.32), (2.46b), (2.46e) and (2.46f) are linear and constraint (2.43), (2.58) and (2.60) are convex. The solution of (P2.2.1) can be obtained by using CVX.

CPU Computation Frequency Allocation
For fixed varying channel relationship coefficient optimization A, transmit power allocation B and local computation allocation D, we formulate the CPU computation frequency allocation problem (P2.3) as

$$(\text{P2.3}): \max_{\{C\},\{\hat{s}_{1,k}[n],\hat{s}_{2,k}[n]\}} \hat{s} \tag{2.62}$$
$$s.t. \quad (2.40), (2.46\text{b})\text{–}(2.46\text{f}).$$

Problem (P2.3) is convex since all of its constraints are linear, which can be solved by using CVX.

Local Computation Allocation
For fixed varying channel relationship coefficient optimization A, transmit power allocation B and CPU computation frequency allocation C, the local computation allocation problem (P2.4) is formulated as

$$(\text{P2.4}): \max_{\{D\},\{\hat{s}_{1,k}[n],\hat{s}_{2,k}[n]\}} \hat{s} \tag{2.63}$$
$$s.t. \quad (2.43), (2.46\text{b})\text{–}(2.46\text{f}).$$

Problem (P2.4) is convex since all of its constraints are linear, e.g., constraint (2.43), (2.46b), (2.46e) and (2.46f) are linear, which can be solved by using CVX.

2.3.3.2 Trajectory Optimization

For fixed varying channel relationship coefficient optimization A, transmit power allocation B, CPU computation frequency allocation C and local computation allocation D, the UAV_S trajectory optimization problem (P3) is re-transformed as

$$(\text{P3}): \max_{\hat{z}\backslash\{q_s[n]\}} \hat{s} \tag{2.64}$$
$$s.t. \quad (2.22), (2.23), (2.24), (2.25), (2.46\text{b})\text{–}(2.46\text{f}).$$

Problem (P3) is hard to handle since constraints (2.25) and (2.46c) are non-convex. We can approximately handle it by SCA technique, in which UAV_S trajectory optimization solution can be obtained by updating it in iterations.

Assume $q_s^r[n]$ represents UAV_S trajectory after r_{th} iteration. We can approximately transform (2.25) into

$$d_{\min}^2 \le 2||q_s^r[n]-q_e[n]||||q_s[n]-|q_s^r[n]||+||q_s^r[n]-q_e[n]||^2, \forall n. \tag{2.65}$$

The right side of (2.46c) is equivalent to

$$\begin{aligned} l\pi_{1,k}[n] = & \log_2\left(\frac{\beta_0 p_k[n]}{H_s^2+||q_s[n]-w_k||^2}+\sum_{l\neq k, l\in\mathcal{K}}\frac{\lambda_{k,l}[n]\beta_0 \dot{p}_l[n]}{H_s^2+||q_s[n]-w_l||^2}+\delta_s^2\right) \\ & -\log_2\left(\sum_{l\neq k, l\in\mathcal{K}}\frac{\lambda_{k,l}[n]\beta_0 p_l[n]}{H_s^2+||q_s[n]-w_l||^2}+\delta_s^2\right). \end{aligned} \tag{2.66}$$

For the first and second item of $\pi_{1,k}[n]$ can be approximately converted as

$$\begin{aligned} lt_{1,k}[n] = & \log_2\left(\frac{\beta_0 p_k[n]}{H_s^2+||q_s^r[n]-w_k||^2}+\sum_{l\neq k, l\in\mathcal{K}}\frac{\lambda_{k,l}[n]\beta_0 p_l[n]}{H_s^2+||q_s^r[n]-w_l||^2}+\delta_s^2\right) \\ & -\frac{\dfrac{\beta_0 p_k[n]\left(||q_s[n]-w_k||^2-||q_s^r[n]-w_k||^2\right)}{\left(H_s^2+||q_s^r[n]-w_k||^2\right)^2}}{\ln 2\left(\dfrac{\beta_0 p_k[n]}{H_s^2+||q_s^r[n]-w_k||^2}+\sum_{l\neq k, l\in\mathcal{K}}\dfrac{\lambda_{k,l}[n]\beta_0 p_l[n]}{H_s^2+||q_s^r[n]-w_l||^2}+\delta_s^2\right)} \\ & -\frac{\sum_{l\neq k, l\in\mathcal{K}}\dfrac{\lambda_{k,l}[n]\beta_0 p_l[n]\left(||q_s[n]-w_l||^2-||q_s^r[n]-w_l||^2\right)}{\left(H_s^2+||q_s^r[n]-w_l||^2\right)^2}}{\ln 2\left(\dfrac{\beta_0 p_k[n]}{H_s^2+||q_s^r[n]-w_k||^2}+\sum_{l\neq k, l\in\mathcal{K}}\dfrac{\lambda_{k,l}[n]\beta_0 p_l[n]}{H_s^2+||q_s^r[n]-w_l||^2}+\delta_s^2\right)}. \end{aligned} \tag{2.67}$$

$$\begin{aligned} lt_{2,k}[n] = & \log_2\left(\sum_{l\neq k, l\in\mathcal{K}}\frac{\lambda_{k,l}[n]\beta_0 p_l[n]}{H_s^2+||q_s^r[n]-w_l||^2}+\delta_s^2\right) \\ & -\frac{2\sum_{l\neq k, l\in\kappa}\dfrac{\lambda_{k,l}[n]\beta_0 p_l[n]\left(||q_s^r[n]-w_l||\right)\left(||q_s[n]-q_s^r[n]||\right)}{\left(H_s^2+||q_s^r[n]-w_l||^2\right)^2}}{\ln 2\left(\sum_{l\neq k, l\in\mathcal{K}}\dfrac{\lambda_{k,l}[n]\beta_0 p_l[n]}{H_s^2+||q_s^r[n]-w_l||^2}+\delta_s^2\right)}. \end{aligned} \tag{2.68}$$

Thus, (2.46c) is approximated as

$$\hat{s}_{1,k}[n] \le t_{1,k}[n] - t_{2,k}[n]. \tag{2.69}$$

Problem (P3) is reformulated as

$$(\text{P3.1}): \max_{\hat{z}\backslash\{q_s[n]\}} \hat{s} \tag{2.70}$$

$$s.t. \quad (2.22), (2.23), (2.24), (2.46b), (2.46d)–(2.46f), (2.65), (2.69).$$

Problem (P3.1) is convex as all its constraints are convex. Then, we can solve it by using CVX in an iterative manner.

2.3.4 *Simulation Results*

In this scenario, five GUs and one GJ are randomly distributed in $400 \times 400\,\text{m}^2$ area. UAV_S takes an optimized trajectory from $q_s^I = [-200, -10, 100]^T$ to $q_s^F = [200, -10, 100]^T$ and UAV_E takes a straight line from $q_e^I = [-200, 50, 100]^T$ to $q_e^F = [200, -60, 100]^T$. We set the reference channel power gain $\beta_0 = -60\,\text{dB}$, Gaussian noise power $\sigma_s^2 = \sigma_e^2 = -110\,\text{dBm}$, GJ transmit power $P_j = 0.1\,\text{W}$, GU_k peak power $P_{\text{max}} = 0.1\,\text{W}$, GU_k average power budget $P_{\text{ave}}^k = 2\,\text{W}$, the required number of CPU computation cycles for computing one bit information at UAV_S and GU_k, $c_s = c_k = 10^3\,\text{cycles/bit}$, GU_k and UAV_S maximum CPU frequency $F_k^{\text{max}} = 1\,\text{GHz}$, $\text{F}_\text{s}^{\text{max}} = 20\,\text{GHz}$ [32], GU_k effective capacitance coefficient $\mathcal{K}_k = 10^{-27}$, the maximum flight speed of UAV_S $V_s^{\text{max}} = 50\,\text{m/s}$, the channel bandwidth $B = 1\,\text{MHz}$ and minimum security computation requirement of each GU $Q_m = 0.5\,\text{Mbits}$.

Figure 2.9 shows the convergence of the average security computation capacity for different flight time T and different GUs transmit peak power P_{max}. We can observe that the proposed scheme has good convergence performance. When T and P_{max} increase, the average security computation capacity of system increases. Figure 2.10 shows the comparison of the optimized UAV_S trajectory and the pre-determined UAV_E trajectory with different flight time T. Figure 2.10a shows the trajectories of UAV_S and UAV_E for NOMA transmission when $T = 10\,\text{s}$. We can observe that UAV_S adjusts its flight trajectory to try to approach GU. However, it cannot hover in the air because T is short and UAV_S needs to reach the end point on time. As shown in Fig. 2.10b, when T becomes large, UAV_S will have enough time to reach the end point. UAV_S will hover in some positions to increase the average security computation capacity of the system.

In order to show the information computation of each GU during the UAVs flight, we compare the security computation capacity of each GU in each slot n for different T in Fig. 2.11. We can observe that the security computation capacity of all the

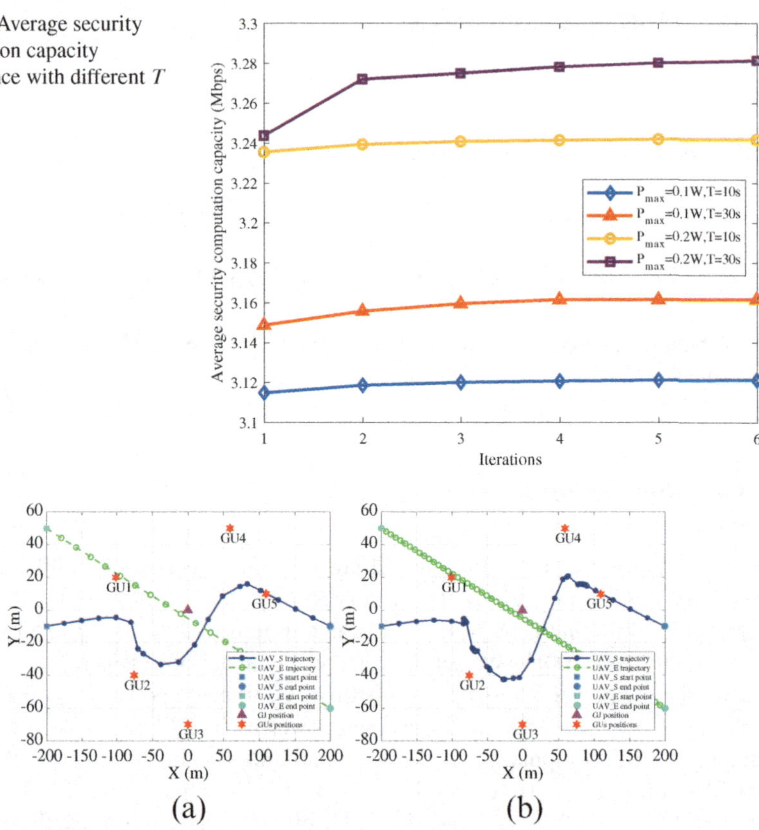

Fig. 2.9 Average security computation capacity convergence with different T and $P_{\max}$

Fig. 2.10 Comparison of UAV_S and UAV_E trajectory with different T. (**a**) UAV_S and UAV_E trajectory with $P_{\max} = 0.1$ W, $T = 10$ s. (**b**) UAV_S and UAV_E trajectory with $P_{\max} = 0.1$ W, $T = 30$ s

GUs are larger than 0.5 Mbits, since the basic security computation needs for each GU Q_m is 0.5 Mbits. UAV_S flies from $[-200, -10, 100]^T$ to $[200, -10, 100]^T$, passing through GU1, GU2, GU3, GU4 and GU5 in turn. When UAV_S approaches GU$_k$, the communication resources and computation resources will be relatively inclined to GU$_k$ to enhance the system's average security computation performance. since GU$_k$ has the best channel condition to UAV_S, the security computation capacity of GU$_k$ is much larger than the other GUs.

Figure 2.12 shows the average security computation capacity of NOMA-based UAV-MEC system versus the peak power $P_{\max}$ with different flight time T. We can observe from Fig. 2.12 that when $P_{\max}$ increases, the average security computation

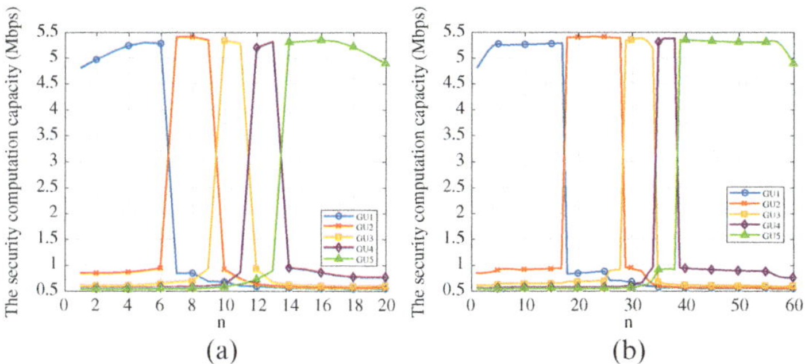

Fig. 2.11 Comparison of the security computation capacity of each GU in slot n with different T. (**a**) $P_{\max} = 0.1$ W, $T = 10$ s. (**b**) $P_{\max} = 0.1$ W, $T = 30$ s

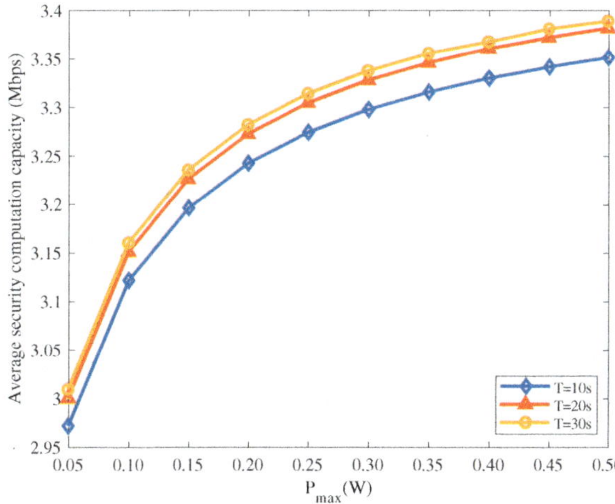

Fig. 2.12 Average security computation capacity variation versus $P_{\max}$ with different T

capacity of the system will also increase, because GUs can obtain more energy to support the transmission of offloading task information with larger $P_{\max}$ (Figs. 2.13 and 2.14).

To prove the superior security computation performance of the proposed scheme, we compare the security calculation performance with the following benchmark schemes in Figs. 2.15 and 2.16.

Scheme 1 The average security computation capacity of the system are maximized by optimizing GU_k local computation, GU_k transmit power, time allocating factor and UAV_S trajectory with TDMA transmission.

Scheme 2 UAV_S flies with straight trajectory, while the varying channel relationship coefficient, GU_k transmit power, GU_k CPU computation frequency, GU_k transmit power and GU_k local computation are optimized to maximize the average security computation capacity of the system.

Scheme 3 The transmit power of GUs are fixed, while the varying channel relationship coefficient, GU_k CPU computation frequency, GU_k local computation

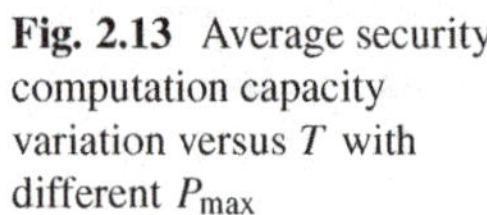

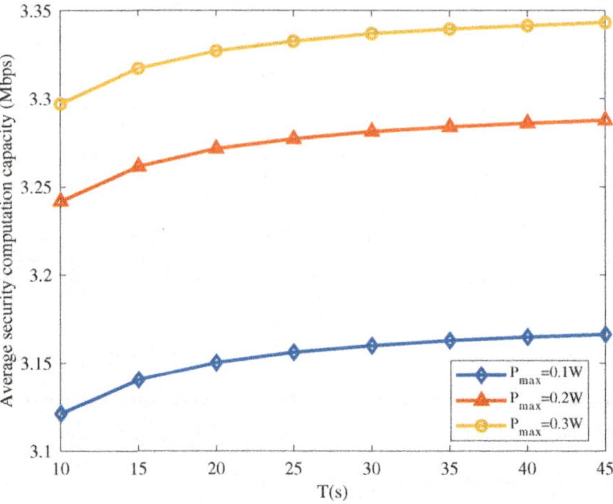

Fig. 2.13 Average security computation capacity variation versus T with different $P_{\max}$

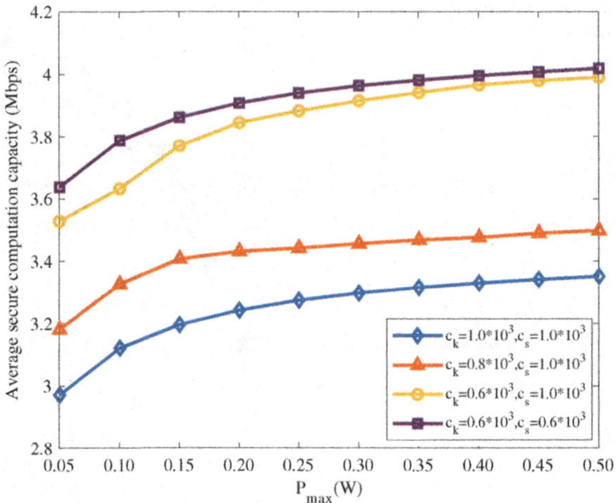

Fig. 2.14 Average security computation capacity variation with different c_s and c_k

and UAV_S trajectory are optimized to maximize the average security computation capacity of the system.

Scheme 4 The security computation capacity of the system is maximized by optimizing UAV_S location, transmit power of GUs, jamming power, offloading ratio, UAV computing capacity and user association [1], in which UAV_S sends jamming signals to enhance security.

In Fig. 2.15, we can find that the security computation performance of the proposed scheme is much better than three benchmark schemes versus T. Compared with scheme 1, the proposed scheme has taken the advantages of NOMA transmission, which permits multi-users to share the same resource. Compared with scheme 2, the proposed scheme also optimizes the trajectory of UAV_S, indicating the importance of trajectory optimization in improving the security computation

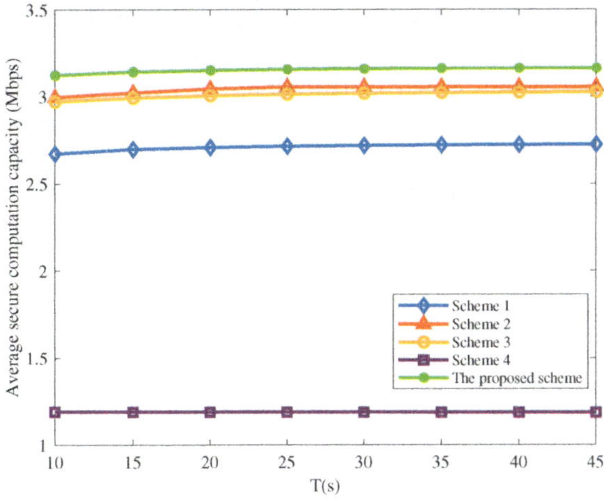

Fig. 2.15 The security computation performance comparison with different schemes versus T

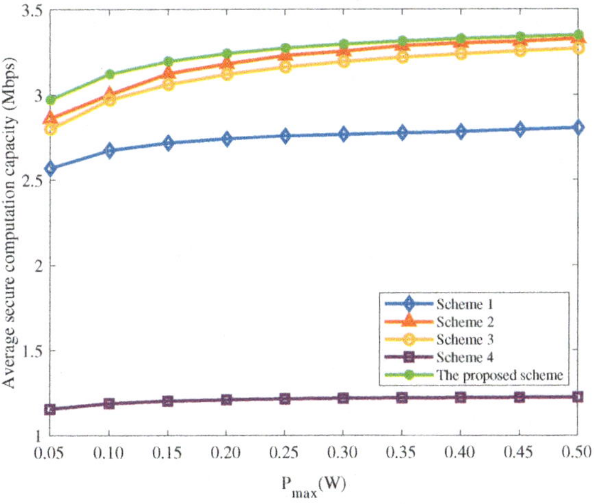

Fig. 2.16 The security computation performance comparison with different schemes versus P_{max}

performance. Compared with scheme 3, the proposed scheme also optimizes the transmit power of GUs, indicating the importance of transmit power allocation in improving the security computation performance. Compared with scheme 4, the proposed scheme has optimized UAV_S trajectory, and UAV_S can fly to assist GUs in computing offloading tasks. Due to the UAVs location are fixed in scheme 4, the average security computation capacity will not change with the change of T.

2.3.5 Summary

In this section, we propose a NOMA-based secure communication scheme. Under the condition of minimum security computation requirements of each GU, we first study the worst security situation through mathematical derivation. Then, we maximize the average security computation capacity of the system via optimizing the varying channel relationship coefficient between the UAV_S and GUs, CPU computation frequency, transmit power, local computation and UAV_S trajectory. We utilize SCA and BCD methods to solve the proposed optimization problem in an iterative manner. The simulation results show that the proposed scheme performs better than the benchmark schemes in terms of the system security computation performance.

References

1. Y. Zhou, C. Pan, P. Yeoh, K. Wang, M. Elkashlan, B. Vucetic, Y. Li, Secure communications for UAV-enabled mobile edge computing systems. IEEE Trans. Commun. **68**(1), 376–388 (2020)
2. Q. Pham, L.B. Le, S. Chung, W. Hwang, Mobile edge computing with wireless backhaul: joint task offloading and resource allocation. IEEE Access **7**, 16444–16459 (2019)
3. W. Lu, P. Si, Y. Gao, H. Han, Z. Liu, Y. Wu, Y. Gong, Trajectory and resource optimization in OFDM based UAV-powered IoT network. IEEE Trans. Green Commun. Netw. **5**(3), 1259–1270 (2021)
4. M. Mozaffari, W. Saad, M. Bennis, M. Debbah, Performance optimization for UAV-enabled wireless communications under flight time constraints, in *GLOBECOM 2017 - 2017 IEEE Global Communications Conference* (2017), pp. 1–6
5. Z. Yu, Y. Gong, S. Gong, Y. Guo, Joint task offloading and resource allocation in UAV-enabled mobile edge computing. IEEE Internet Things J. **7**(4), 3147–3159 (2020)
6. F. Zhou, Y. Wu, R.Q. Hu, Y. Qian, Computation rate maximization in UAV-enabled wireless-powered mobile-edge computing systems. IEEE J. Sel. Areas Commun. **36**(9), 1927–1941 (2018)
7. Y. Du, K. Yang, K. Wang, G. Zhang, Y. Zhao, D. Chen, Joint resources and workflow scheduling in UAV-enabled wirelessly-powered MEC for IoT systems. IEEE Trans. Veh. Technol. **68**(10), 10187–10200 (2019)
8. Y. Wang, Z.-Y. Ru, K. Wang, P.-Q. Huang, Joint deployment and task scheduling optimization for large-scale mobile users in multi-UAV-enabled mobile edge computing. IEEE Trans. Cybern. **50**(9), 3984–3997 (2020)
9. Y. Liu, S. Xie, Y. Zhang, Cooperative offloading and resource management for UAV-enabled mobile edge computing in power IoT system. IEEE Trans. Veh. Technol. **69**(10), 12229–12239 (2020)
10. Q. Hu, Y. Cai, G. Yu, Z. Qin, M. Zhao, G.Y. Li, Joint offloading and trajectory design for UAV-enabled mobile edge computing systems. IEEE Internet Things J. **6**(2), 1879–1892 (2019)
11. J. Zhang, L. Zhou, F. Zhou, B. Seet, H. Zhang, Z. Cai, J. Wei, Computation-efficient offloading and trajectory scheduling for multi-UAV assisted mobile edge computing. IEEE Trans. Veh. Technol. **69**(2), 2114–2125 (2020)
12. W. Liu, Y. Xu, D. Wu, H. Wang, X. Zheng, X. Chen, Distributed energy-efficient and secure offloading in air-to-ground MEC networks. EURASIP J. Adv. Signal Process. **2021**(1), 71 (2021)
13. Z. Ding, P. Fan, H.V. Poor, Impact of non-orthogonal multiple access on the offloading of mobile edge computing. IEEE Trans. Commun. **67**(1), 375–390 (2019)
14. H. Lei, C. Zhu, K.-H. Park, W. Lei, I.S. Ansari, T.A. Tsiftsis, On secure NOMA-based terrestrial and aerial IoT systems. IEEE Internet Things J. https://doi.org/10.1109/JIOT.2021
15. H. Lei, R. Gao, K.-H. Park, I.S. Ansari, K.J. Kim, M.-S. Alouini, On secure downlink NOMA systems with outage constraint. IEEE Trans. Commun. **68**(12), 7824–7836 (2020)

16. A. Abushattal, S. Althunibat, M. Qaraqe, H. Arslan, A secure downlink NOMA scheme against unknown internal eavesdroppers. IEEE Wirel. Commun. Lett. **10**(6), 1281–1285 (2021)
17. F. Cui, Y. Cai, Z. Qin, M. Zhao, G.Y. Li, Multiple access for mobile-UAV enabled networks: joint trajectory design and resource allocation. IEEE Trans. Commun. **67**(7), 4980–4994 (2019)
18. Z. Na, Y. Liu, J. Shi, C. Liu, Z. Gao, UAV-supported clustered NOMA for 6G-enabled Internet of things: trajectory planning and resource allocation. IEEE Internet Things J. **8**(20), 15041–15048 (2020)
19. S. Li, B. Li, W. Zhao, Joint optimization of caching and computation in multi-server NOMA-MEC system via reinforcement learning. IEEE Access **8**, 112762–112771 (2020)
20. Y. Wu, K. Ni, C. Zhang, L.P. Qian, D.H.K. Tsang, NOMA-assisted multi-access mobile edge computing: a joint optimization of computation offloading and time allocation. IEEE Trans. Veh. Technol. **67**(12), 12244–12258 (2018)
21. F. Guo, H. Zhang, H. Ji, X. Li, V.C.M. Leung, Joint trajectory and computation offloading optimization for UAV-assisted MEC with NOMA, in *IEEE Conference on Computer Communications Workshops (INFOCOM WKSHPS 2018)* (2019), pp. 1–6
22. X. Zhang, J. Zhang, J. Xiong, L. Zhou, J. Wei, Energy-efficient multi-UAV-enabled multiaccess edge computing incorporating NOMA. IEEE Internet Things J. **7**(6), 5613–5627 (2020)
23. I. Budhiraja, N. Kumar, S. Tyagi, S. Tanwar, Energy consumption minimization scheme for NOMA-based mobile edge computation networks underlaying UAV. IEEE Syst. J. **15**(4), 5724–5733 (2021)
24. N. Rupasinghe, Y. Yapici, I. Güvenc, H. Dai, A. Bhuyan, Enhancing physical layer security for NOMA transmission in mmWave drone networks, in *2018 52nd Asilomar Conference on Signals Systems and Computers* (2018), pp. 729–733
25. G. Mu, Security efficiency maximization for multi-UAV–aided network with mobile edge computing. Front. Comput. Sci. **3**, 691854. https://doi.org/10.3389/fcomp.2021
26. A. Singh, M.R. Bhatnagar, R.K. Mallik, Physical layer security of a multiantenna-based CR network with single and multiple primary users. IEEE Trans. Veh. Technol. **66**(12), 11011–11022 (2017)
27. Y. Ai, A. Mathur, M. Cheffena, M.R. Bhatnagar, H. Lei, Physical layer security of hybrid satellite-FSO cooperative systems. IEEE Photonics J. **11**(1), 1–14 (2019)
28. Z. Sheng, H.D. Tuan, A.A. Nasir, T.Q. Duong, H.V. Poor, Secure UAV-enabled communication ssing Han–Kobayashi signaling. IEEE Trans. Wirel. Commun. **19**(5), 2905–2919 (2020)
29. Y. Cao, N. Zhao, Y. Chen, M. Jin, Z. Ding, Y. Li, F.R. Yu, Secure transmission via beamforming optimization for NOMA networks. IEEE Wirel. Commun. **27**(1), 193–199 (2020)
30. X. Sun, W. Yang, Y. Cai, Secure communication in NOMA-assisted millimeter-wave SWIPT UAV networks. IEEE Internet Things J. **7**(3), 1884–1897 (2020)
31. B. Duo, J. Luo, Y. Li, H. Hu, Z. Wang, Joint trajectory and power optimization for securing UAV communications against active eavesdropping. China Commun. **18**(1), 88–99 (2021)
32. Y. Xu, T. Zhang, D. Yang, Y. Liu, M. Tao, Joint resource and trajectory optimization for security in UAV-assisted MEC systems. IEEE Trans. Commun. **69**(1), 573–588 (2021)
33. S. Li, B. Duo, M.D. Renzo, M. Tao, X. Yuan, Robust secure UAV communications with the aid of reconfigurable intelligent surfaces. IEEE Trans. Wirel. Commun. **20**(10), 6402–6417 (2021)

Chapter 3
RIS-Based Secure Communications for UAV-Enabled MEC Systems

With the progress of the IoT and wireless communications, various intelligent applications, including smart homes, augmented reality, and autonomous systems, have significantly improved the quality of users' experiences. At the same time, these advancements have led to a substantial surge in the volume of data generated by GUs, creating new challenges for devices in terms of their storage and computational capabilities.

MEC offers a promising approach to reduce the workload on GUs by enabling them to offload computationally intensive tasks to nearby edge servers. This approach reduces processing latency and enhances overall efficiency. However, MEC systems still face limitations, especially in scenarios with remote or infrastructure-scarce regions, where coverage and resource availability are restricted. By leveraging the dynamic mobility of UAVs, integrating UAVs into MEC systems can effectively address these challenges, offering more flexible and efficient computational resources to GUs.

To further enhance communication and computation efficiency, RISs are increasingly employed in UAV-enabled MEC systems. RISs consist of numerous reflecting elements that can dynamically adjust the phase and amplitude of reflected signals, improving communication quality. These surfaces can help mitigate signal degradation caused by obstacles, providing a reliable solution to enhance the overall performance of systems.

Despite these advancements, the LoS transmission characteristics of RIS-based UAV-enabled MEC systems leave them vulnerable to interception by malicious eavesdroppers. This poses a significant threat to the confidentiality of offloaded tasks and compromises the security of transmitted information. As a result, improving the secure performance of systems remains a critical challenge. It should be noted that current research primarily addresses threats from stationary ground eavesdroppers, often neglecting the potential danger posed by UAVs acting as aerial eavesdroppers.

In this chapter, we consider two RIS-based UAV-enabled MEC systems for secure communication. In the RIS-based UAV-enabled MEC system, UAV server

W. Lu et al., *Secure Communications in Unmanned Aerial Vehicle-Enabled Mobile Edge Computing Systems*, SpringerBriefs in Computer Science,
https://doi.org/10.1007/978-981-96-9611-6_3

(UAV_S) equipped with a MEC server is employed to assist GUs in computation, and a RIS on the wall to enhance transmission quality. And in the UAV-RIS-Relaying MEC system, UAV equipped with a RIS to enhance the communication quality, and a ground base station with muti-antenna for transmitting information. Our objective is to enhance the secure communication performance of two systems while guaranteeing the task processing capacity requirements of all GUs. The main contributions of this chapter are summarized as follows

- First, a joint resource and trajectory optimization scheme is thoroughly investigated for secure enhancement in a RIS-based UAV-enabled MEC system with coexisting of a malicious UAV eavesdropper. The proposed scheme maximizes the minimum secrecy capacity among all GUs in the system by optimizing time allocation, transmit power, local computation CPU frequency, RIS phase shifts, and UAV trajectory, while satisfying the GUs' task processing capacity requirements. Given the non-convexity of this problem, we solve it by dividing it into several subproblems and alternately optimizing them using the BCD, SCA, and phase alignment methods.
- Then, we investigate a UAV-RIS-Relaying MEC system, considering the limitations on the UAV flight area, base station transmission power, and RIS phase shifts. By jointly optimizing the UAV position, base station beamforming, and RIS phase shifts, the minimum secrecy rate of the system is maximized. Then we divide this optimization problem into two optimization sub-problems. The non-convex terms in the sub-problems are addressed using the first-order Taylor expansion, which converts the original non-convex sub-problems into convex optimization problems.
- Finally, The simulation results indicate that both of our proposed schemes significantly enhance the secure communication performance of the RIS-based UAV-enabled MEC system compared to the benchmark schemes.

The subsequent sections of this chapter are structured as follows: Sect. 3.1 provides a review of related studies. We present the scheme of the RIS-based resource and trajectory optimization for secure communications in Sect. 3.2, with system model, problem formulation, solution development, the simulation results of this part, and corresponding summary. Then, we present the scheme of the RIS-based secure communications for UAV-relaying MEC systems in Sect. 3.3, with system model, problem formulation, solution development, the simulation results of this part, and corresponding summary.

3.1 Related Studies

MEC allows GUs to transfer their computationally demanding tasks to edge servers, facilitating efficient data processing, thereby increasing computation capacity and reducing latency [1]. Bi et al. investigated multi-user MEC systems with dynamic channels and stochastic task arrivals to improve data processing while ensuring long-term queue stability and power efficiency [2]. UAVs, with their mobility, enhance coverage and offer flexible deployment, especially in environments with infrastructure limitations [3–5]. Bian et al. improved the anti-jamming capability of UAV-assisted wireless data collectionby tackling the issue of multiple jammer attacks under the condition of imperfect CSI [5]. Integrating UAV into MEC networks can effectively address the shortcomings of MEC by providing flexible and on-demand computational resources [6–9]. Ding et al. decreased the total weighted energy consumption of a secure UAV-enabled MEC system by proposing a collaborative communication and computation scheme [6]. Han et al. reduced the task delay of a UAV-MEC system by jointly considering user association and UAV deployment [7]. Wang et al. extended UAV operating time and associated network lifetime through joint region partitioning and UAV trajectory scheduling in a UAV-enabled MEC network [8]. Liu et al. aimed to minimize energy consumption in a MISO UAV-assisted MEC system by jointly optimizing the UAV's beamforming vectors, CPU frequency, and trajectory, along with the UEs' transmission power and CPU frequency [9].

Meanwhile, RISs dynamically adjust reflected signals to mitigate obstacles and improve communication quality [10, 11]. Shen et al. focused on maximizing the system's secrecy rate under the source transmit power constraint and the unit modulus constraints on phase shifts in RIS-assisted multi-antenna systems [11]. RIS-based UAV-enabled MEC systems are generally classified into two categories. The first places the RIS on a wall [12–16], Qin et al. enhanced energy efficiency in RIS-assisted UAV-MEC systems by jointly optimizing resource allocation, phase shift design, and the UAV's trajectory [14]. Wang et al. improved communication performance in multi-UAV-MEC systems through the joint optimization of offloading strategies, UAV trajectories, and phase shift configurations [15]. Mei et al. aimed to maximize the energy efficiency of RIS-assisted UAV systems by jointly optimizing the UAV's trajectory, task offloading, caching decisions, and the RIS phase-shift design [16]. The second mounts the RIS on the UAV [17–21], Zhai et al. jointly optimized UAV trajectory, RIS passive beamforming and MEC resource allocation to maximize the energy efficiency of the system [19]. Liao et al. reduced RUAVs energy by jointly considering TUAV hovering altitude, RIS phase-shift vector, RUAV service selection indicator, and RUAVs turning points [20]. Duo et al. improved the energy efficiency of an ARIS- and AMEC-assisted MEC system by jointly optimizing the trajectories of two UAVs, the ARIS phase shifts, the computation offloading strategy, and the allocation of computational resources [21]. However, the integration of these technologies in RIS-based UAV-enabled MEC systems still faces challenges in ensuring secure communications, as information transmission remains vulnerable to interception.

To ensure the security of systems, resource allocation schemes have been proposed [22–25]. Gu et al. optimized computational resources, RIS phase shifts, and UAV trajectories to enhance energy-efficient security [22]. Zhou et al. improved secure computing by optimizing resource allocation, RIS phase shifts, and UAV placement [23]. Michailidis et al. enhanced secure computation efficiency in MEC-enabled IoT networks through the joint optimization of transmit power allocation, time slot scheduling, task distribution, and the phase shift design of the RIS [24]. Gao et al. expanded secure computation capacity in RIS-assisted UAV-MEC systems by jointly optimizing the IRS phase shifts, communication and computing resource allocation, and the UAV's trajectory [25].

3.2 RIS-Based Resource and Trajectory Optimization for Secure Communications

3.2.1 System Model for RIS-Based UAV-Enabled MEC Systems

We focus on a RIS-based UAV-enabled MEC system to ensure secure communications, which involves a UAV server (UAV_S), a UAV eavesdropper (UAV_E), K GUs, and an RIS, as depicted in Fig. 3.1. Both UAVs and GUs are configured with single antennas.

Consider that GUs possess computation-intensive tasks requiring processing. Due to the constrained computational power of GUs, a UAV_S equipped with an MEC server is introduced to support their computation tasks. At the same time, UAV_E, following a predefined trajectory, attempts to intercept the offloaded tasks from GUs. To enhance communication security, an RIS mounted on a building is employed to boost transmission quality, making task offloading for GUs more effective.

The flight duration of UAVs, denoted as T, is divided into N discrete time slots, with each time slot represented as $\delta_t = T/N$. During the n-th time slot, where $n \in \{1, \ldots, N\}$, the horizontal position of UAV_i for $i \in \{\text{S}, \text{E}\}$ is expressed as $q_i[n] = \left[x_i, y_i\right]^T$. The altitude of each UAV_i remains constant at z_i.

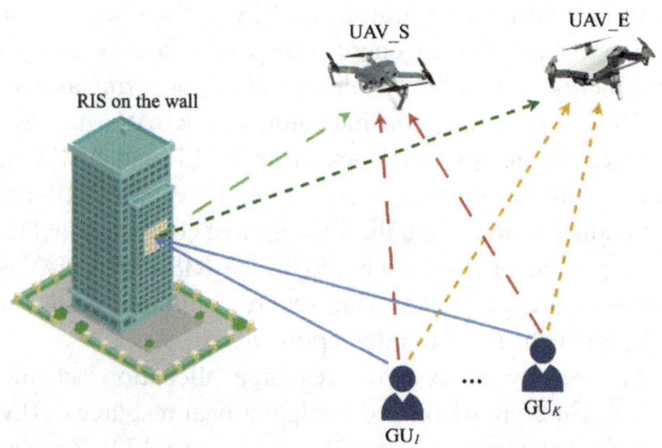

Fig. 3.1 A RIS-based UAV-enabled MEC system

UAV_S is assumed to have prior knowledge of the locations of all GUs as well as the channel state information. The movement of UAV_S is constrained by

$$q_s[1] = q_s^I, q_s[N] = q_s^F, \tag{3.1}$$

$$\|q_s[n+1] - q_s[n]\| \leq \delta_t V_s^{\max}, n = 1, 2, \ldots, N-1, \tag{3.2}$$

where q_s^I is the initial location of UAV_S, q_s^F are final location of UAV_S, and V_s^{max} is the maximum flight speed of UAV_S.

3.2.2 Problem Formulation for Secure Capacity Maximization

Each time slot δ_t is further divided into K subslots, denoted by $\tau_k[n], k \in \{1, \ldots, K\}$, where $\tau_k[n]$ represents the proportion of time allocated to the k-th GU for task offloading. Then, we have

$$\textstyle\sum_{k=1}^{K} \tau_k[n] \leq 1, \tag{3.3}$$

$$0 \leq \tau_k[n] \leq 1. \tag{3.4}$$

The horizontal coordinates of the k-th GU are given as $w_k = \left[x_k, y_k\right]^T$. The RIS is configured as a uniform linear array with L reflecting elements, using the first element as the reference point, and its horizontal position is described by $w_r = \left[x_r, y_r\right]^T$ with a height of h_r. For the k-th subslot in the n-th time slot, the reflection matrix is expressed as $\Phi_k[n] = \text{diag}\left\{e^{j\theta_{1k}[n]}, \ldots, e^{j\theta_{lk}[n]}, \ldots, e^{j\theta_{Lk}[n]}\right\}$, where $\theta_{lk}[n]$ denotes the phase shift of the l-th element, which should satisfy

$$0 \leq \theta_{lk}[n] \leq 2\pi. \tag{3.5}$$

3.2.2.1 Communication Model

The channels in the system are dominated by LoS links. Then, the channel gains from UAV_i to the k-th GU, from UAV_i to RIS, from RIS to the k-th GU is given by

$$h_{i,k}[n] = \sqrt{\beta_0 d_{i,k}^{-\alpha}[n]}, \tag{3.6}$$

$$h_{i,r}[n] = \sqrt{\beta_0 d_{i,r}^{-\alpha}[n]}\left[1, e^{-j\frac{2\pi d}{\lambda}\phi_{i,r}[n]}, \ldots, e^{-j\frac{2(L-1)\pi d}{\lambda}\phi_{i,r}[n]}\right]^T, \tag{3.7}$$

$$h_{r,k} = \sqrt{\beta_0 d_{r,k}^{-\alpha}}\left[1, e^{-j\frac{2\pi d}{\lambda}\phi_{r,k}}, \ldots, e^{-j\frac{2(L-1)\pi d}{\lambda}\phi_{r,k}}\right]^T, \tag{3.8}$$

where β_0 is the channel power gain at 1 m, α is the path-loss exponent, $d_{i,k}[n]$ and $d_{i,r}[n]$ are the distance of UAV_i to the k-th GU and RIS in the n-th time slot, respectively, λ is the carrier wavelength, d is the distance of adjacent reflecting elements of RIS, $\phi_{i,r} = \frac{x_r - x_i[n]}{d_{i,r}[n]}$ is the sine of the angles-of-departure of RIS-UAV_i.

Let the transmit power of the k-th GU be represented as $p_k[n]$. The achievable transmission rate from the k-th GU to UAV_i is given by

$$R_{i,k}[n] = \log_2\left(1 + \frac{p_k[n]\left|h_{i,k}[n] + h_{r,k}^H \Phi_k[n] h_{i,r}[n]\right|^2}{\sigma_i^2}\right), \tag{3.9}$$

where σ_i^2 is the power of Gaussian noise at UAV_i.

Then, the secrecy rate of the kth GU is given by

$$R_{\text{sec},k}[n] = \left[R_{s,k}[n] - R_{e,k}[n]\right]^+, \tag{3.10}$$

where $[x]^+ = \max(x, 0)$.

3.2.2.2 Computing Model

We adopt a partial offloading strategy for task computation, where each GU is capable of executing local computation and data transmission simultaneously. Let c_k denote the CPU cycles required by the k-th GU to process each bit, and $f_{\text{loc},k}$ represent the local computation CPU frequency during the nth time slot. The local computation capacity and secure offloading capacity for the k-th GU are defined as

$$C_{\text{loc},k}[n] = \delta_t f_{\text{loc},k}[n], \tag{3.11}$$

$$C_{\text{off},k}[n] = c_k \tau_k[n] \delta_t B R_{\text{sec},k}[n], \tag{3.12}$$

where B is bandwidth.

The computation capacity of UAV_S cannot exceed to its capability,

$$C_{\text{off},k}[n] \le \delta_t \tau_k[n] F_s^{\max}, \tag{3.13}$$

where $F_s^{\max}$ is the maximum CPU frequency of UAV_S.

To ensure the minimum task processing requirement of GUs Q_m, we have

$$C_{\text{loc},k}[n] + C_{\text{off},k}[n] \ge Q_m. \tag{3.14}$$

Thus, based on the partial offloading strategy, the secrecy capacity of the kth GU during T is determined as

$$C_{k,\text{sec}} = \frac{1}{T}\sum_{n=1}^{N}\left(C_{\text{loc},k}[n] + C_{\text{off},k}[n]\right). \tag{3.15}$$

In the n-th time slot, the energy consumption of local computation of the k-th GU is $\delta_t\sigma f_{\text{loc},k}^3[n]$, where σ is the effective capacitance coefficient. The transmit energy consumption is $\tau_k[n]\delta_t p_k[n]$. Then, we can obtain

$$\frac{1}{T}\sum_{n=1}^{N}\left(\delta_t\sigma f_{\text{loc},k}^3[n] + \tau_k[n]\delta_t p_k[n]\right) \le P_k^{\text{ave}}, \tag{3.16}$$

where P_k^{ave} is the maximum average energy consumption of the k-th GU.

3.2.2.3 Problem Formulation

Our goal is to maximize minimum secrecy capacity by jointly optimizing time allocation $\boldsymbol{\tau} = \{\tau_k[n]\}$, transmit power $\boldsymbol{P} = \{p_k[n]\}$, local computation CPU frequency $\boldsymbol{F} = \{f_{\text{loc},k}[n]\}$, RIS phase shifts $\boldsymbol{\Phi} = \{\Phi_k[n]\}$ and UAV_S trajectory $\boldsymbol{Q} = \{q_s[n]\}$. The optimization problem can be written to

$$(\text{P1}): \max_{\{\boldsymbol{\tau},\boldsymbol{P},\boldsymbol{F},\boldsymbol{\Phi},\boldsymbol{Q}\}} \min_{\forall k} C_{k,\text{sec}} \tag{3.17a}$$

$$s.t.\quad (3.1)\text{–}(3.5),\ (3.13),\ (3.14),\ (3.16)$$

$$\|q_s[n] - q_e[n]\|^2 \ge d_{\min}^2, \tag{3.17b}$$

$$0 \le p_k[n] \le P_k^{\max}, \tag{3.17c}$$

$$f_{\text{loc},k}[n] \le F_k^{\max}, \tag{3.17d}$$

where (3.17b) indicates the UAV collision avoidance constraint, (3.17c) indicates the transmission power constraint for each GU in each time slot, (3.17d) indicates the local computation frequency constraint of each GU, $F_k^{\max}$ is the maximum CPU frequency of the k-th GU.

It should be noted that optimization problem (P1) is a complex non-convex problem, which is difficult to solve directly.

3.2.3 *Problem Solution*

To solve (P1), we first introduce the auxiliary variable x, $x_{1,k}[n]$, $x_{2,k}[n]$ to simplify it as

$$(\text{P2}): \max_{\{\boldsymbol{\tau},\boldsymbol{P},\boldsymbol{F},x_{1,k}[n],x_{2,k}[n]\}} x \tag{3.18a}$$

$$s.t. \quad (3.1)\text{–}(3.5), (3.16), (3.17b)\text{–}(3.17d)$$

$$x \le \frac{1}{T}\sum_{n=1}^{N}\left(\delta_t f_{\mathrm{loc},k}[n] + c_k\tau_k[n]\delta_t B\left(x_{1,k}[n] - x_{2,k}[n]\right)\right), \tag{3.18b}$$

$$x_{1,k}[n] \le \log_2\left(1 + \frac{p_k[n]\left|H_{s,k}[n]\right|^2}{\sigma_s^2}\right), \tag{3.18c}$$

$$x_{2,k}[n] \ge \log_2\left(1 + \frac{p_k[n]\left|H_{e,k}[n]\right|^2}{\sigma_e^2}\right), \tag{3.18d}$$

$$c_k B\left(x_{1,k}[n] - x_{1,k}[n]\right) \le F_s^{\max}, \tag{3.18e}$$

$$\delta_t f_{\mathrm{loc},k}[n] + c_k\tau_k[n]\delta_t B\left(x_{1,k}[n] - x_{2,k}[n]\right) \ge Q_m, \tag{3.18f}$$

where x, $x_{1,k}[n]$, $x_{2,k}[n]$ represent the lower bound of the objective function and the achievable rate of the k-th GU-UAV_S, the upper bound of the achievable rate of the k-th GU-UAV_E, respectively, $H_{i,k}[n] = h_{i,k}[n] + h_{r,k}^H\Phi_k[n]h_{i,r}[n](i \in \{\mathrm{S}, \mathrm{E}\})$.

Next, the optimization problem can be solved by optimizing the block structure of the variables through the following five steps.

3.2.3.1 Step 1: Optimizing $\boldsymbol{\tau}$ with Giving $\boldsymbol{P}$, $\boldsymbol{F}$, $\boldsymbol{\Phi}$, $\boldsymbol{Q}$

With transmit power, local computation CPU frequency, phase shifts, and trajectory fixed, optimization problem (P2) can be reformulated as

$$(\mathrm{P3}): \quad \max_{\{\boldsymbol{\tau}, x_{1,k}[n], x_{2,k}[n]\}} \quad x \tag{3.19a}$$

$$s.t. \quad (3.3), (3.4), (3.16), (3.18b)\text{–}(3.18f).$$

Due to the linear nature of the constraints, (P3) represents a standard convex optimization problem. Therefore, it can be addressed using convex optimization tools like CVX [26].

3.2.3.2 Step 2: Optimizing $\boldsymbol{P}$ with Giving $\boldsymbol{\tau}$, $\boldsymbol{F}$, $\boldsymbol{\Phi}$, $\boldsymbol{Q}$

With time allocation, local computation CPU frequency, phase shifts, and trajectory fixed, optimization problem (P2) is reformulated as

$$(\mathrm{P4}): \quad \max_{\{\boldsymbol{P}, x_{1,k}[n], x_{2,k}[n]\}} \quad x \tag{3.20a}$$

$$s.t. \quad (3.16), (3.17c), (3.18b)\text{–}(3.18f).$$

It can be observed that (3.18c) and (3.18d) are non-convex. To address this, (3.20) is approximated as a convex problem using the SCA technique, where transmit power is iteratively updated.

Note that the convex function can be derived through a global lower bound obtained via the first-order Taylor expansion [27]. In the rth iteration, let $p_k^{(r)}[n]$ represent the transmit power of the kth GU. With this, (3.18c) and (3.18d) can be reformulated as

$$x_{1,k}[n] \le \log_2\left(1 + \frac{p_k^{(r)}[n]\left|H_{s,k}[n]\right|^2}{\sigma_s^2}\right) + \frac{\left|H_{s,k}[n]\right|^2}{\ln 2}\frac{p_k[n] - p_k^{(r)}[n]}{\sigma_s^2 + p_k^{(r)}[n]\left|H_{s,k}[n]\right|^2}, \tag{3.21}$$

$$x_{2,k}[n] \le \log_2\left(1 + \frac{p_k^{(r)}[n]\left|H_{e,k}[n]\right|^2}{\sigma_e^2}\right) + \frac{\left|H_{e,k}[n]\right|^2}{\ln 2}\frac{p_k[n] - p_k^{(r)}[n]}{\sigma_e^2 + p_k^{(r)}[n]\left|H_{e,k}[n]\right|^2}. \tag{3.22}$$

Then, optimization problem (P4) can be approximately converted into a convex problem, and the convex optimization techniques can be used.

3.2.3.3 Step 3: Optimizing F with Giving τ, P, Φ, Q

With time allocation, transmit power, phase shifts, and trajectory fixed, optimization problem (3.18) can be rewritten as

$$(\text{P5}): \max_{\{F, x_{1,k}[n], x_{2,k}[n]\}} \quad x \tag{3.23a}$$

$$s.t. \quad (3.16), (3.17\text{d}), (3.18\text{b})\text{–}(3.18\text{f}).$$

Note that optimization problem (P5) is a convex problem, which is readily solvable applying convex optimization techniques.

3.2.3.4 Step 4: Optimizing Φ with Giving τ, P, F, Q

With time allocation, local computation CPU frequency, transmit power, and trajectory fixed, $h_{r,k}^H \Phi_k[n] h_{s,r}[n]$ is given by

$$h_{r,k}^H \Phi_k[n] h_{s,r}[n] = \frac{\beta_0 \sum_{l=1}^{L} e^{j\theta_{lk}[n] - j\frac{2(L-1)\pi d}{\lambda}(\phi_{r,k} + \phi_{s,r}[n])}}{\sqrt{d_{r,k}^{\alpha} d_{s,r}^{\alpha}[n]}}. \tag{3.24}$$

Next, the phase alignment method is utilized to optimize the phase shifts. When the reflected signals from different RIS elements are phase-aligned, they combine coherently to maximize the received signal power, thereby enhancing the secrecy capacity [4]. To achieve this, the total phase of the reflected link for each RIS element is set equal to that of the direct link. Consequently, the RIS phase shift $\theta_{lk}[n]$ can be optimized as

$$\theta_{lk}[n] = \arg(h_{s,k}[n]) + \frac{2(L-1)\pi d}{\lambda}(\phi_{r,k} + \phi_{s,r}[n]), \tag{3.25}$$

where $\arg(\cdot)$ is the phase of the channel.

Substituting (3.25) into (3.24), we can obtain the optimal $\Phi_k[n]$.

3.2.3.5 Step 5: Optimizing $\boldsymbol{Q}$ with Giving $\boldsymbol{\tau}$, $\boldsymbol{P}$, $\boldsymbol{F}$, $\boldsymbol{\Phi}$

With time allocation, local computation CPU frequency, transmit power, and phase shifts fixed, optimization problem (P2) can be rewritten as

$$(\text{P6}): \max_{\{\boldsymbol{Q},x_{1,k}[n],x_{2,k}[n]\}} x \tag{3.26a}$$

$$s.t. \quad (3.1), (3.2), (3.17b), (3.18b), (3.18d)–(3.18f)$$

$$x_{1,k}[n] \le \log_2\left(1 + \frac{p_k[n]}{\sigma_s^2}\left|\frac{\beta_0}{d_{s,k}^{\frac{\alpha}{2}}[n]} + \frac{A_k}{d_{s,r}^{\frac{\alpha}{2}}[n]}\right|^2\right), \tag{3.26b}$$

where $A_k = \frac{e^{j\arg(h_{s,k}[n])}\beta_0 L}{\sqrt{d_{r,k}^{\alpha}}}$.

Note that (3.17b) and (3.26b) are still non-convex. In the r-th iteration, define $\boldsymbol{Q}^{(r)}$=$\{q_s^{(r)}$[n]$\}$ as the trajectory of UAV_S, (3.17b) can be approximately transformed to

$$\left\|q_s^{(r)}[n] - q_e[n]\right\|^2 + 2\left\|q_s^{(r)}[n] - q_e[n]\right\| \|q_s[n] - q_e[n]\| \ge d_{\min}^2. \tag{3.27}$$

We introduce the slack variables $v_k[n]$ and $z_k[n]$ to solve (3.26b). Problem (P6) can be equivalently transformed as

$$(\text{P6.1}): \max_{\{\boldsymbol{Q},x_{1,k}[n],x_{2,k}[n],v_k[n],z_k[n]\}} x \tag{3.28a}$$

$$s.t. \quad (3.1),(3.2), (3.18b), (3.18d)–(3.18f),(3.27)$$

$$x_{1,k}[n] \le \log_2\left(1 + \frac{p_k[n]}{\sigma_s^2}\left|\frac{\beta_0}{v_k[n]} + \frac{A_k}{z_k[n]}\right|^2\right), \tag{3.28b}$$

$$v_k^{\frac{2}{\alpha}}[n] \ge d_{s,k}[n], \tag{3.28c}$$

$$z_k^{\frac{2}{\alpha}}[n] \ge d_{s,r}[n], \tag{3.28d}$$

where $v_k[n]$ and $z_k[n]$ represent the upper bound of the distance of UAV_S to the k-th GU and RIS, respectively.

It can be demonstrated by applying the Hessian criterion that the constraint (3.28b) represents a convex function with respect to $v_k[n]$ and $z_k[n]$. Therefore, (3.28b)–(3.28d) can be addressed by using the same SCA method as outlined in step 2. At the point $v_k^{(r)}[n]$ and $z_k^{(r)}[n]$, we have

$$x_{1,k}[n] \leq \log_2 A_0[\mathrm{n}] + \frac{B_0[n]}{A_0[n]\ln 2}(v_k[n] - v_k^{(r)}[n]) + \frac{C_0[n]}{A_0[n]\ln 2}(z_k[n] - z_k^{(r)}[n]), \tag{3.29}$$

$$d_{s,k}[n] \leq \left(v_k^{(r)}[n]\right)^{\frac{2}{\alpha}} + \frac{2}{\alpha}\left(v_k^{(r)}[n]\right)^{\frac{2}{\alpha}-1}\left(v_k[n] - v_k^{(r)}[n]\right), \tag{3.30}$$

$$d_{s,r}[n] \leq \left(z_k^{(r)}[n]\right)^{\frac{2}{\alpha}} + \frac{2}{\alpha}\left(z_k^{(r)}[n]\right)^{\frac{2}{\alpha}-1}\left(z_k[n] - z_k^{(r)}[n]\right), \tag{3.31}$$

where $A_0[n] = 1 + \frac{p_k[n]}{\sigma_s^2}\left(\frac{\beta_0^2}{\left(v_k^{(r)}[n]\right)^2} + \frac{A_k^2}{\left(z_k^{(r)}[n]\right)^2} + \frac{2\beta_0 A_k}{v_k^{(r)}[n] z_k^{(r)}[n]}\right)$,

$$B_0[n] = -\frac{p_k[n]}{\sigma_s^2}\left(\frac{2\beta_0^2}{\left(v_k^{(r)}[n]\right)^3} + \frac{2\beta_0 A_k}{\left(v_k^{(r)}[n]\right)^2 z_k^{(r)}[n]}\right),$$

$$C_0[n] = -\frac{p_k[n]}{\sigma_s^2}\left(\frac{2A_k^2}{\left(z_k^{(r)}[n]\right)^3} + \frac{2\beta_0 A_k}{v_k^{(r)}[n](z_k^{(r)}[n])^2}\right).$$

Then, we can approximately convert optimization problem (P6.1) as

$$(\text{P6.2}): \quad \max_{\{Q, x_{1,k}[n], x_{2,k}[n], v_k[n], z_k[n]\}} \quad x \tag{3.32a}$$

$$s.t. \quad (3.1),(3.2), (3.18b), (3.18d)–(3.18f),(3.27),(3.29),(3.30),(3.31).$$

As a convex optimization problem, optimization problem (P6.2) can be efficiently solved using standard convex optimization techniques.

In conclusion, (P2) can be solved by optimizing the block structure of the variables into several sub-problems. We can solve the problems (P3), (P4), and (P5) to update the solution of $\boldsymbol{\tau}$, $\boldsymbol{P}$, and $\boldsymbol{F}$. Then, we can solve the problem Eq. 3.25 by using the phase alignment method to update the optimized values of $\boldsymbol{\Phi}$, and solve the problem (P6.2) to update the solution of $\boldsymbol{Q}$. With these variables are optimized by updating in an alternating manner, we can finally obtain a high-quality solution of (OP2). The complexity of the algorithm depends on $(3KN + N)$ optimal variables, yielding a computational complexity of $IO(KN^{3.5})\log_2(1/\varepsilon)$, where I represents the number of iterations [3].

3.2.4 Simulation Results

In this section, the performance of the proposed scheme is validated through simulation results. GUs are randomly distributed in a $400 \times 400\,\mathrm{m}^2$ area. UAV_S flies at a constant speed from $\left[-200, -10\right]^T$ to $\left[200, -10\right]^T$ with the altitude of 100 m, and UAV_E flies from $\left[200, 50\right]^T$ to $\left[200, -60\right]^T$ at an altitude of 100 m. We randomly set $w_r = \left[0, -80\right]^T$, $B = 1\,\mathrm{MHz}$, $\delta_t = 0.5\,\mathrm{s}$, $\beta_0 = -60\,\mathrm{dB}$, $\sigma_s^2 = \sigma_e^2 = -120\,\mathrm{dBm}$, $F_s^{\max} = 10\,\mathrm{GHz}$, $F_k^{\max} = 1\,\mathrm{GHz}$, $P_k^{\max} = 20\,\mathrm{dBm}$, $P_k^{\mathrm{ave}} = 1\,\mathrm{W}$, $c_k = 1000$ cycles/bit, $\sigma = 10^{-27}$, $Q_{\mathrm{m}} = 0.1$ Mbits. The following results are all based on the default setting of $K = 5$, $L = 100$, $T = 20\,\mathrm{s}$, $P_k^{\max} = 0.2\,\mathrm{W}$.

Figure 3.2 shows the relationship between the minimum secrecy capacity of our system and the number of RIS reflecting elements L under varying $P_k^{\max}$ and flight period T. As L increases, the minimum secrecy capacity also increases, attributed to the larger array gains provided by additional reflecting elements, which enhance the system's security performance. Moreover, higher maximum transmit power of GU and longer UAV_S flight time lead to improved minimum secrecy capacity.

Figure 3.3 depicts the minimum secrecy capacity as a function of the number of GUs for different schemes. Specifically, Scheme 1 optimizes only the RIS phase shifts, while Scheme 2 excludes optimization of both RIS phase shifts and UAV_S trajectory. With an increasing number of GUs, the minimum secrecy capacity declines due to the reduced average service time per GU. Notably, the

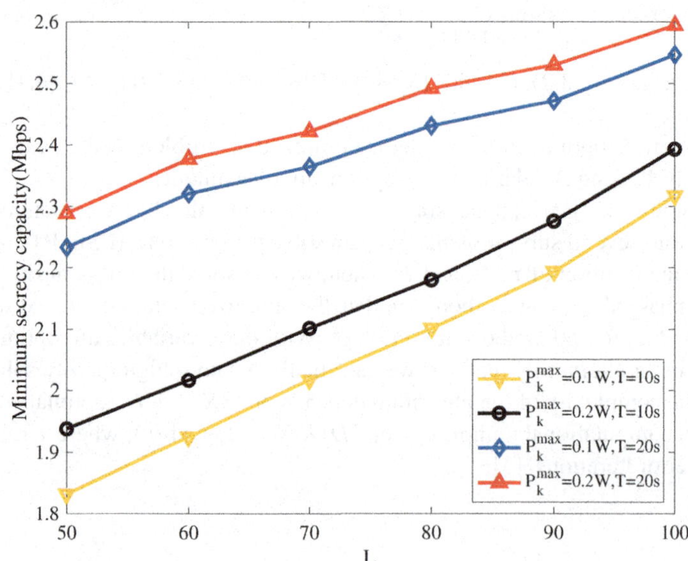

Fig. 3.2 Minimum secrecy capacity versus L with different $P_k^{\max}$ and T

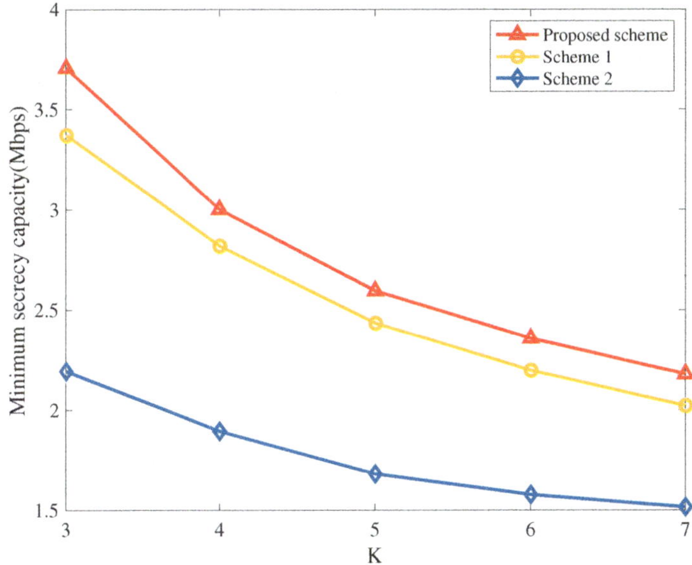

Fig. 3.3 Minimum secrecy capacity versus K with different schemes

proposed scheme outperforms the others, highlighting the effectiveness of the joint optimization algorithm.

Figure 3.4 demonstrates the convergence behavior of the proposed scheme for different values of L and T. The minimum secrecy capacity stabilizes after a few iterations, confirming the good convergence properties of the proposed scheme.

3.2.5 Summary

This section introduces a joint optimization scheme for resource allocation and trajectory design to enhance the security performance of the RIS-based UAV-enabled MEC system. In this setup, UAV_E intercepts data transmission from GUs to UAV_S, while the RIS facilitates signal transmission. The proposed approach aims to maximize the minimum secrecy capacity across all GUs by optimizing time allocation, transmit power, local computation CPU frequency, RIS phase shifts, and UAV_S trajectory, all while meeting the task processing requirements of the GUs. To tackle the non-convex nature of the problem, mathematical techniques are employed to simplify it into a more tractable form and decompose it into several sub-problems. These sub-problems are then solved iteratively using phase alignment and SCA methods. Simulation results validate that the proposed scheme significantly enhances the security performance of the RIS-based UAV-enabled MEC system.

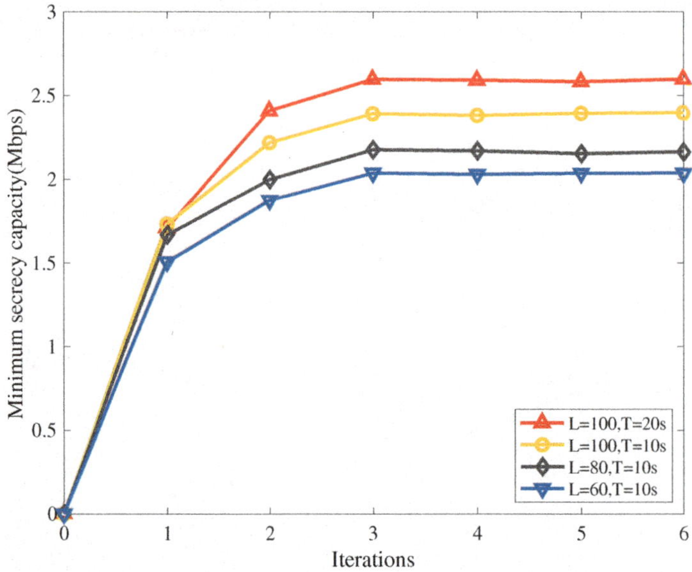

Fig. 3.4 Minimum secrecy capacity versus iterations with different L and T

3.3 RIS-Based Secure Communications for UAV-Relaying MEC Systems

3.3.1 System Model for UAV-RIS-Relaying MEC Systems

As shown in Fig. 3.5, the UAV-RIS-Relaying MEC system includes one base station(BS), one UAV equipped with a RIS, K legitimate users, and one eavesdropper. The BS is equipped with M antennas, and the RIS is composed of a uniform linear array with N reflecting elements, with each phase of element controlled by the UAV [28]. It is assumed that the direct link from the BS to the users is blocked by obstacles, so communication between the BS and users is relayed through the UAV. The BS transmits data to all users over the same frequency band, while the eavesdropper attempts to eavesdrop on the data of all legitimate users at any time. Assuming that the BS has perfect CSI for all links. The eavesdropper and users are located on the ground, with their horizontal positions denoted as $w_e[n] = \left[x_e, y_e\right]^T$ and $w_k[n] = \left[x_k, y_k\right]^T, k \in \{1, \ldots, K\}$, respectively. The horizontal position of the BS is $w_b[n] = \left[x_b, y_b\right]^T$, with height H_b. The UAV has a fixed height H, and its horizontal position is $w_u[n] = \left[x_b, y_b\right]^T$.

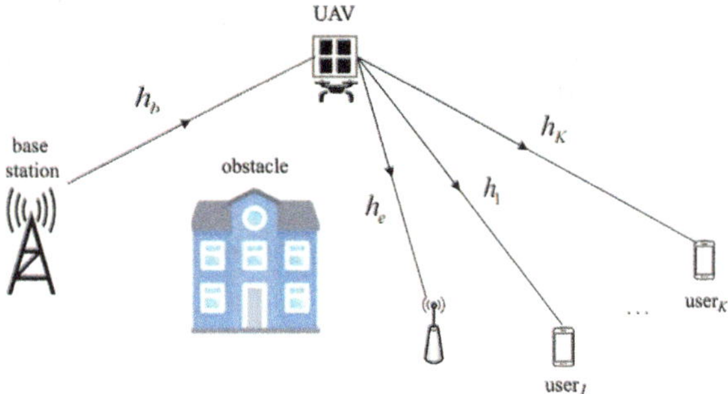

Fig. 3.5 A UAV-RIS-Relaying MEC system

3.3.2 Problem Formulation for Secure Rate Maximization

3.3.2.1 Communication Model

Assuming that the channels in the system are dominated by LoS channels, the channel gain from the UAV to user k can be expressed as $h_k = \sqrt{\beta_0 d_k^{-\alpha}} g_k$, where β_0 is the channel power gain at 1 m, α is the path-loss exponent, d_k is the distance of UAV to the user k, and

$$g_k = \left[1, e^{-j\frac{2\pi d}{\lambda}\phi_k}, \ldots, e^{-j\frac{2(N-1)\pi d}{\lambda}\phi_k}\right]^T, \tag{3.33}$$

where λ is the carrier wavelength, d is the distance of adjacent reflecting elements of RIS, $\phi_k = \frac{x_u - x_k}{d_k}$ is the cosine of the angles-of-departure of the signal at UAV.

The channel gain from the UAV to eavesdropper can be expressed as $h_e = \sqrt{\beta_0 d_e^{-\alpha}} g_e$, where d_e is the distance of UAV to the eavesdropper, and

$$g_e = \left[1, e^{-j\frac{2\pi d}{\lambda}\phi_e}, \ldots, e^{-j\frac{2(N-1)\pi d}{\lambda}\phi_e}\right]^T, \tag{3.34}$$

where $\phi_e = \frac{x_u - x_e}{d_e}$ is the cosine of the angles-of-departure of the signal at UAV.

The channel gain from the UAV to BS can be expressed as $h_b = \sqrt{\beta_0 d_b^{-\alpha}} g_N g_M^H$, where d_b is the distance of UAV to BS, and

$$g_N = \left[1, e^{-j\frac{2\pi d}{\lambda}\phi_N}, \ldots, e^{-j\frac{2(N-1)\pi d}{\lambda}\phi_N}\right]^T, \tag{3.35}$$

$$g_M = \left[1, e^{-j\frac{2\pi d}{\lambda}\phi_M}, \ldots, e^{-j\frac{2(N-1)\pi d}{\lambda}\phi_M}\right]^T, \tag{3.36}$$

where ϕ_N and ϕ_M represent the cosine of the angle-of-deviation of the signal at BS and the angle-of-arrival at UAV, respectively.

The BS employs linear precoding as the beamforming vector, denoted as $\omega_k \in \mathbb{C}^{M\times 1}$. Assuming the data transmitted by the BS to user k is s_k, the total transmitted signal from the BS is $x = \sum_{i=1}^{K} \omega_i s_i$. The received signals at user k and the eavesdropper are given by

$$y_k = \left(h_k^H \Phi h_b\right) \sum_{i=1}^{K} \omega_i s_i + n_k, \tag{3.37}$$

$$y_e = \left(h_e^H \Phi h_b\right) \sum_{i=1}^{e} \omega_i s_i + n_e, \tag{3.38}$$

where $\Phi = \text{diag}\left\{e^{j\theta_1}, \ldots, e^{j\theta_N}\right\}$ is the RIS phase shift matrix, n_k and n_e is Gaussian noise with zero mean and variance δ at user k and the eavesdropper, respectively.

Thus, the achievable transmission rate at user k and the eavesdropper are given by

$$r_k = \log_2\left(1 + \frac{\left|\left(h_k^H \Phi h_b\right) \omega_k\right|^2}{\sum_{i\neq k}^{K} \left|\left(h_k^H \Phi h_b\right) \omega_i\right|^2 + \sigma^2}\right), \tag{3.39}$$

$$r_{e,k} = \log_2\left(1 + \frac{\left|\left(h_e^H \Phi h_b\right) \omega_k\right|^2}{\sum_{i\neq k}^{K} \left|\left(h_e^H \Phi h_b\right) \omega_i\right|^2 + \sigma^2}\right). \tag{3.40}$$

3.3.2.2 Problem Formulation

We aim to maximize the minimum secrecy rate among all users by jointly optimizing the UAV position $\boldsymbol{w}_u$, the BS beamforming vector $\boldsymbol{W} = [\omega_1, \ldots, \omega_K]$, and the RIS phase shifts Φ. The optimization problem can be formulated as

$$(\text{P1}): \max_{\boldsymbol{w}_u, \boldsymbol{W}, \Phi} \min_k \{r_k - r_{e,k}\} \tag{3.41a}$$

$$s.t. \quad 0 \le x_u \le X,\ 0 \le y_u \le Y, \tag{3.41b}$$

$$\sum_{i=1}^{K} \|\omega_i\|^2 \le P, \tag{3.41c}$$

$$\theta_n \in [0, 2\pi], \tag{3.41d}$$

where (3.41b) indicates that the UAV is placed within a certain area, (3.41c) indicates the upper limit of the transmission power P of BS, and (3.41d) indicates the phase shift constraint for each reflecting element of the RIS.

3.3.3 Problem Solution

Due to the non-convex nature of the objective function, directly solving the optimization problem (P1) is challenging. Therefore, the optimization problem is decomposed into two sub-problems: UAV position optimization, and BS beamforming and RIS phase shifts optimization. By using the first-order Taylor expansion, the non-convex sub-problems are transformed into convex problems, and an alternating optimization approach is used to solve them. first, we assume that the BS beamforming vector and RIS phase shifts are known, and optimize the UAV position. Then, with the UAV position determined, the BS beamforming vector and RIS phase shifts are optimized accordingly.

3.3.3.1 Step 1: Optimizing $\boldsymbol{w}_u$ with Fixed $\boldsymbol{W}, \boldsymbol{\Phi}$

With $\boldsymbol{W}$ and Φ fixed, the optimization problem (3.6) can be converted into

$$(\text{P2}): \max_{\boldsymbol{w}_u} \min_{k} \{r_k - r_{e,k}\} \tag{3.42a}$$

$$s.t. \quad 0 \le x_u \le X,\ 0 \le y_u \le Y. \tag{3.42b}$$

Since the objective function is non-convex, to facilitate handling it, we firstly have

$$r_k = \log_2\left(1 + \frac{A_k}{d_k^\alpha d_b^\alpha + B_k}\right), \tag{3.43}$$

$$r_{e,k} = \log_2\left(1 + \frac{C_k}{d_e^\alpha d_b^\alpha + D_k}\right). \tag{3.44}$$

where $A_k = \frac{\beta_0^2 |(g_k^H \Phi g_N g_M^H)\omega_k|^2}{\sigma^2}$, $B_k = \frac{\beta_0^2 \sum_{i \neq k}^K |(g_k^H \Phi g_N g_M^H)\omega_i|^2}{\sigma^2}$, $C_k = \frac{\beta_0^2 |(g_e^H \Phi g_N g_M^H)\omega_k|^2}{\sigma^2}$, $D_k = \frac{\beta_0^2 \sum_{i \neq k}^K |(g_e^H \Phi g_N g_M^H)\omega_i|^2}{\sigma^2}$.

Due to the non-convexity of the $d_k^\alpha d_b^\alpha$ and $d_e^\alpha d_b^\alpha$, we introduce the relaxation variable $\boldsymbol{Z} = z_k, \boldsymbol{V} = v_k, k \in 1, \dots, K$. Then, (P2) can be transformed as

$$(\text{P2.1}): \max_{\boldsymbol{w}_u, \boldsymbol{Z}, \boldsymbol{V}} \min_{k} \{\widehat{r_k} - \widehat{r_{e,k}}\} \tag{3.45a}$$

$$s.t. \quad 0 \leq x_u \leq X, \ 0 \leq y_u \leq Y, \tag{3.45b}$$

$$z_k^{\frac{\alpha}{2}} \geq d_k^2 d_b^2 + B_k, \tag{3.45c}$$

$$v_k^{\frac{\alpha}{2}} \geq d_e^2 d_b^2 + D_k, \tag{3.45d}$$

where $\widehat{r_k} = \log 2(1 + \frac{z_k}{A_k})$, $\widehat{r_{e,k}} = \log 2(1 + \frac{v_k}{C_k})$.

Note that A_k, B_k, C_k, and D_k are complex functions of $\boldsymbol{w}_u$, we replace A_k, B_k, C_k, and D_k with their upper bounds $\widehat{A_k}$, $\widehat{B_k}$, $\widehat{C_k}$, and $\widehat{D_k}$

$$\begin{aligned} A_k &= \frac{\beta_0^2 |(g_k^H \Phi g_N g_M^H)\omega_k|^2}{\sigma^2} \leq \frac{\beta_0^2 |(g_k^H \Phi g_N g_M^H)|^2 |\omega_k|^2}{\sigma^2} \\ &= \frac{\beta_0^2 \left| \sum_{m=1}^M \sum_{n=1}^N \sum_{t=1}^N e^{j\theta_t - j\pi d \frac{(n-1)}{\lambda}(\phi_N + \phi_k) + \frac{(m-1)}{\lambda}\phi_M} \right|^2 |\omega_k|^2}{\sigma^2} \leq \frac{\beta_0^2 M N^2 |\omega_k|^2}{\sigma^2} \triangleq \widehat{A_k}, \end{aligned} \tag{3.46}$$

$$\begin{aligned} B_k &= \frac{\beta_0^2 \left|(g_k^H \Phi g_N g_M^H)\, \omega_i\right|^2}{\sigma^2} \leq \frac{\beta_0^2 \left|(g_k^H \Phi g_N g_M^H)\right|^2 \sum_{i \neq k}^K |\omega_i|^2}{\sigma^2} \\ &= \frac{\beta_0^2 \left| \sum_{m=1}^M \sum_{n=1}^N \sum_{t=1}^N e^{j\theta_t - j\pi d \frac{(n-1)}{\lambda}(\phi_N + \phi_k) + \frac{(m-1)}{\lambda}\phi_M} \right|^2 \sum_{i \neq k}^K |\omega_i|^2}{\sigma^2} \\ &\leq \frac{\beta_0^2 M N^2 \sum_{i \neq k}^K |\omega_i|^2}{\sigma^2} \triangleq \widehat{B_k}, \end{aligned} \tag{3.47}$$

$$\begin{aligned} C_k &= \frac{\beta_0^2 |(g_e^H \Phi g_N g_M^H)\omega_k|^2}{\sigma^2} \leq \frac{\beta_0^2 |(g_e^H \Phi g_N g_M^H)|^2 |\omega_k|^2}{\sigma^2} \\ &= \frac{\beta_0^2 \left| \sum_{m=1}^M \sum_{n=1}^N \sum_{t=1}^N e^{j\theta_t - j\pi d \frac{(n-1)}{\lambda}(\phi_N + \phi_e) + \frac{(m-1)}{\lambda}\phi_M} \right|^2 |\omega_k|^2}{\sigma^2} \leq \frac{\beta_0^2 M N^2 |\omega_k|^2}{\sigma^2} \triangleq \widehat{C_k}, \end{aligned} \tag{3.48}$$

$$\begin{aligned} D_k &= \frac{\beta_0^2 \left|(g_e^H \Phi g_N g_M^H)\, \omega_i\right|^2}{\sigma^2} \leq \frac{\beta_0^2 \left|(g_e^H \Phi g_N g_M^H)\right|^2 \sum_{i \neq k}^K |\omega_i|^2}{\sigma^2} \\ &= \frac{\beta_0^2 \left| \sum_{m=1}^M \sum_{n=1}^N \sum_{t=1}^N e^{j\theta_t - j\pi d \frac{(n-1)}{\lambda}(\phi_N + \phi_e) + \frac{(m-1)}{\lambda}\phi_M} \right|^2 \sum_{i \neq k}^K |\omega_i|^2}{\sigma^2} \\ &\leq \frac{\beta_0^2 M N^2 \sum_{i \neq k}^K |\omega_i|^2}{\sigma^2} \triangleq \widehat{D_k}. \end{aligned} \tag{3.49}$$

It is observed that this objective function in (P2.1) is still non-convex, we replace $\widehat{r_k}$ with its lower bound $\widehat{r_k}^b$ using a first-order Taylor expansion,

$$\widehat{r}_k = \log_2\left(1+\frac{\widehat{A}_k}{z_k}\right) \geq \log_2\left(1+\frac{\widehat{A}_k}{z_k^{(l)}}\right) + \frac{-\widehat{A}_k(z_k - z_k^{(l)})}{z_k^{(l)}\left(z_k^{(l)}+\widehat{A}_k\right)\ln 2} \triangleq \widehat{r}_k^b. \tag{3.50}$$

To handle the non-convexity of the constraint (3.45c) and (3.54d), the non-convex term $d_k^2 + d_b^2$ and $d_e^2 + d_b^2$ are expanded by using first-order Taylor approximation,

$$\begin{aligned} d_k^2 d_b^2 &= \tfrac{1}{2}\left((d_k^2+d_b^2)^2 - (d_k^4+d_b^4)\right) \leq \tfrac{1}{2}\left((d_k^2+d_b^2)^2 - (d_k^{(l)^4}+d_b^{(l)^4})\right) \\ &\quad -2(d_k^{(l)^2})(\boldsymbol{w}_u^{(l)} - \boldsymbol{W}_k)^T(\boldsymbol{w}_u - \boldsymbol{w}_u^{(l)}) - 2(d_b^{(l)^2})(\boldsymbol{w}_u^{(l)} - \boldsymbol{W}_b)^T(\boldsymbol{w}_u - \boldsymbol{w}_u^{(l)}) \\ &\triangleq f_k(\boldsymbol{w}_u), \end{aligned} \tag{3.51}$$

$$\begin{aligned} d_e^2 d_b^2 &= \tfrac{1}{2}\left((d_e^2+d_b^2)^2 - (d_e^4+d_b^4)\right) \geq \tfrac{1}{2}\left(\left((d_e^{(l)})^2+(d_b^{(l)})^2\right)^2 - (d_e^4+d_b^4)\right) \\ &\quad +2(d_e^{(l)})^2(2\boldsymbol{w}_u^{(l)} - \boldsymbol{W}_e - \boldsymbol{W}_b)^T(\boldsymbol{w}_u - \boldsymbol{w}_u^{(l)}) \\ &\quad +2(d_b^{(l)})^2(2\boldsymbol{w}_u^{(l)} - \boldsymbol{W}_e - \boldsymbol{W}_b)^T(\boldsymbol{w}_u - \boldsymbol{w}_u^{(l)}) \triangleq f_e(\boldsymbol{w}_u), \end{aligned} \tag{3.52}$$

where $d_k^{(l)}$, $d_e^{(l)}$, $d_b^{(l)}$ and $\boldsymbol{w}_u^{(l)}$ represent the distances between the UAV and the user, distances between the UAV and the eavesdropper, distances between the UAV and the BS, and the UAV position at the lth iteration.

Since $v_k^{\frac{\alpha}{2}}$ in constraint (3.54d) is a concave function, the constraint is not feasible in the optimization process. Therefore, $v_k^{\frac{\alpha}{2}}$ is replaced by its first-order Taylor expansion using the value from the previous iteration, $v_k^{(l)}$. Then, we have

$$v_k^{\frac{\alpha}{2}} \leq \left(v_k^{(l)}\right)^{\frac{2}{\alpha}} + \frac{2}{\alpha}\left(v_k^{(l)}\right)^{\frac{2}{\alpha}-1}\left(v_k - v_k^{(l)}\right) \triangleq \widehat{v}_k. \tag{3.53}$$

Thus, (P2.1) can be transformed as

$$(\text{P2.2}):\ \max_{\boldsymbol{w}_u,\boldsymbol{Z},\boldsymbol{V}}\ \min_k\{r_k^b - \widehat{r_{e,k}}\} \tag{3.54a}$$

$$s.t.\quad 0 \leq x_u \leq X,\ 0 \leq y_u \leq Y, \tag{3.54b}$$

$$z_k^{\frac{\alpha}{2}} \geq f_k(\boldsymbol{w}_u) + \widehat{B}_k, \tag{3.54c}$$

$$\widehat{v}_k \leq f_e(\boldsymbol{w}_u) + \widehat{D}_k. \tag{3.54d}$$

The optimization problem (P2.2) is a convex optimization problem and can be solved using the convex optimization techniques such as CVX.

3.3.3.2 Step 2: Optimizing W, Φ with Fixed w_u

With w_u fixed, the optimization problem (P1) can be converted into

$$\text{(P3)} : \max_{W,\Phi} \min_{k} \{r_k - r_{e,k}\} \tag{3.55a}$$

$$s.t. \quad \sum_{i=1}^{K} \|\omega_i\|^2 \le P, \tag{3.55b}$$

$$\theta_n \in [0, 2\pi]. \tag{3.55c}$$

Note that objective function is non-convex, it is challenging to solve the optimization problem directly. We simplify the objective function into a more manageable form. first, we rewrite the channel and RIS phase shifts. Let $H_k = \text{diag}(h_k^H h_b)$, $H_e = \text{diag}(h_e^H h_b)$, $\mathbf{v} = [e^{j\theta_1}, \ldots, e^{j\theta_N}]^T$, $b_k(W, \mathbf{v}) = \sum_{i \ne k}^{K} \left|\mathbf{v}^H H_k \omega_i\right|^2 + \sigma^2$, $b_e(W, \mathbf{v}) = \sum_{i \ne k}^{K} \left|\mathbf{v}^H H_e \omega_i\right|^2 + \sigma^2$. The achievable rate at user k and the eavesdropping rate at the eavesdropper can be rewritten as

$$r_k = \log_2 \left(1 + \frac{\left|\mathbf{v}^H H_k \omega_k\right|^2}{b_k(W, \mathbf{v})}\right), \tag{3.56}$$

$$r_{e,k} = \log_2 \left(1 + \frac{\left|\mathbf{v}^H H_e \omega_k\right|^2}{b_{e,k}(W, \mathbf{v})}\right). \tag{3.57}$$

To address the non-convexity of the objective function, we replace r_k with its lower bound and $r_{e,k}$ with its upper bound, respectively.

When $0 \le y \le |x|^2$, we have

$$\begin{aligned}
\log_2 \left(1 + \frac{|x|^2}{y}\right) &\ge \log_2 \left(1 + \frac{|\bar{x}|^2}{\bar{y}}\right) + \nabla_x \log_2 \left(1 + \frac{|\bar{x}|^2}{\bar{y}}\right)(x - \bar{x}) \\
&\quad + \nabla_y \log_2 \left(1 + \frac{|\bar{x}|^2}{\bar{y}}\right)(y - \bar{y}) \\
&= \log_2 \left(1 + \frac{|\bar{x}|^2}{\bar{y}}\right) + \frac{2\Re\{\bar{x}x\}}{\bar{y}\ln 2} \\
&\quad - \frac{|\bar{x}|^2}{\bar{y}(\bar{y} + |\bar{x}|^2)\ln 2}(y + |x|^2) - \frac{|\bar{x}|^2}{\bar{y}\ln 2},
\end{aligned} \tag{3.58}$$

where $x = \mathbf{v}^H H_k \omega_k$, $y = b_k(W, \mathbf{v})$, $\bar{x} = (\mathbf{v}^{(l)})^H H_k \omega_k^{(l)}$, and $\bar{y} = b_k(W^{(l)}, \mathbf{v}^{(l)})$. By substituting these values, we can obtain the lower bound of r_k,

$$r_k = \log_2\left(1+\frac{|\mathbf{v}^H H_k\omega_k|^2}{b_k(\mathbf{W},\mathbf{v})}\right) \geq \log_2\left(1+\frac{\left|(\mathbf{v}^{(l)})^H H_k\omega_k^{(l)}\right|^2}{b_k(\mathbf{W}^{(l)},\mathbf{v}^{(l)})}\right)+\frac{2\Re\left\{(\mathbf{v}^{(l)})^H H_k\omega_k^{(l)}\mathbf{v}^H H_k\omega_k\right\}}{b_k(\mathbf{W}^{(l)},\mathbf{v}^{(l)})\ln 2}$$
$$-\frac{\left|(\mathbf{v}^{(l)})^H H_k\omega_k^{(l)}\right|^2}{b_k(\mathbf{W}^{(l)},\mathbf{v}^{(l)})\left(b_k(\mathbf{W}^{(l)}\mathbf{v}^{(l)})+\left|(\mathbf{v}^{(l)})^H H_k\omega_k^{(l)}\right|^2\right)\ln 2}\left(b_k(\mathbf{W},\mathbf{v})+\left|\mathbf{v}^H H_k\omega_k\right|^2\right)$$
$$-\frac{\left|(\mathbf{v}^{(l)})^H H_k\omega_k^{(l)}\right|^2}{b_k(\mathbf{W}^{(l)}\mathbf{v}^{(l)})\ln 2} \triangleq R_k, \tag{3.59}$$

R_k is a jointly concave function with respect to $\mathbf{W}$ and $\mathbf{v}$. That is, R_k is concave with respect to $\mathbf{v}$ when $\mathbf{W}$ is fixed, and R_k is concave with respect to $\mathbf{W}$ when $\mathbf{v}$ is fixed.

Since $\log_2(1+z)$ is a concave function with respect to z, we have

$$\log_2(1+z) \leq \log_2(1+\bar{z}) + \frac{(z-\bar{z})}{(1+\bar{z})\ln 2}, \tag{3.60}$$

substituting $z=\frac{|\mathbf{v}^H H_e\omega_k|^2}{b_{e,k}(\mathbf{W},\mathbf{v})}$, $\bar{z}=\frac{\left|(\mathbf{v}^{(l)})^H H_e\omega_k^{(l)}\right|^2}{b_{e,k}(\mathbf{W}^{(l)},\mathbf{v}^{(l)})}$ into Eq. (3.58), we can obtain

$$r_{e,k} = \log_2\left(1+\frac{|\mathbf{v}^H H_e\omega_k|^2}{b_{e,k}(\mathbf{W},\mathbf{v})}\right)$$
$$\leq \log_2\left(1+\frac{\left|(\mathbf{v}^{(l)})^H H_e\omega_k^{(l)}\right|^2}{b_{e,k}(\mathbf{W}^{(l)},\mathbf{v}^{(l)})}\right)+\frac{\left|(\mathbf{v}^{(l)})^H H_e\omega_k^{(l)}\right|^2}{b_{e,k}(\mathbf{W}^{(l)},\mathbf{v}^{(l)})\ln 2}\times\left(\ln 2+\frac{\left|(\mathbf{v}^{(l)})^H H_e\omega_k^{(l)}\right|^2}{b_{e,k}(\mathbf{W}^{(l)},\mathbf{v}^{(l)})}\right)^{-1}$$
$$\overset{(a)}{\leq} \log_2\left(1+\frac{\left|(\mathbf{v}^{(l)})^H H_e\omega_k^{(l)}\right|^2}{b_{e,k}(\mathbf{W}^{(l)},\mathbf{v}^{(l)})}\right)+\frac{\left|(\mathbf{v}^{(l)})^H H_e\omega_k^{(l)}\right|^2}{b_{e,k}(\mathbf{W}^{(l)},\mathbf{v}^{(l)})\ln 2}\times\left(\ln 2+\frac{\left|(\mathbf{v}^{(l)})^H H_e\omega_k^{(l)}\right|^2}{b_{e,k}(\mathbf{W}^{(l)},\mathbf{v}^{(l)})}\right)^{-1}$$
$$\triangleq R_{e,k}, \tag{3.61}$$

where $b_e(\omega,\mathbf{v},\omega^{(t)},\mathbf{v}^{(t)}) = \sum_{i\neq k}^K \Re\left\{(\omega_i^{(t)})^H G_e^H \mathbf{v}^{(t)} \times\left(2\mathbf{v}^H G_e\omega_i-(\mathbf{v}^{(t)})^H G_e\omega_i^{(t)}\right)\right\}+\sigma^2$. The inequality (a) holds because $b_e(\omega,\mathbf{v},\omega^{(t)},\mathbf{v}^{(t)})$ is derived via the first-order Taylor expansion of $b_e(\mathbf{W},\mathbf{v})$ at the point $\mathbf{W}^{(l)}$ and $\mathbf{v}^{(l)}$, resulting in $b_e(\mathbf{W},\mathbf{v}) \geq b_e(\omega,\mathbf{v},\omega^{(t)},\mathbf{v}^{(t)})$. Thus, R_k is concave with respect to $\mathbf{v}$ and $\mathbf{W}$.

Based on Eqs. (3.59) and (3.61), the optimization problem (P3) can be reformulated as

$$(\text{P3.1}) : \max_{\mathbf{W},\mathbf{v}} \min_k \{R_k - R_{e,k}\} \tag{3.62a}$$
$$s.t.\quad (3.55\text{b}), (3.55\text{c})$$

The objective function of (P3.1) is non-convex because of the coupling between the variables $\boldsymbol{W}$ and $\mathbf{v}$. And R_k is jointly concave with respect to $\boldsymbol{W}$ and $\mathbf{v}$, while $R_{e,k}$ is jointly convex with respect to these variables. Therefore, the objective function of (P3.1) is also jointly concave in $\boldsymbol{W}$ or $\mathbf{v}$, allowing us to decompose (P3.1) into two sub-problems, (P3.2) and (P3.3), and solve them using alternating optimization,

$$(\text{P3.2}): \max_{\boldsymbol{W}} \min_{k} \{R_k - R_{e,k}\} \tag{3.63a}$$

$$s.t. \quad \sum_{i=1}^{K} \|\omega_i\|^2 \leq P, \tag{3.63b}$$

$$(\text{P3.3}): \max_{\mathbf{v}} \min_{k} \{R_k - R_{e,k}\} \tag{3.64a}$$

$$s.t. \quad \theta_n \in [0, 2\pi]. \tag{3.64b}$$

Both sub-problems are convex optimization problems and can be solved using the convex optimization techniques such as CVX.

3.3.4 Simulation Results

In this section, the performance of the proposed scheme is verified through simulation results. First, the BS is set at a horizontal position of $\left[0, 0\right]^T$ with a height of 20 m. User 1 is located at $\left[10, 100\right]^T$, user 2 at $\left[20, 80\right]^T$, and the eavesdropper at $\left[80, 0\right]^T$. Both users and the eavesdropper are located on the ground. Other parameter settings are: $P = 10\,\text{dBm}$, $H = 50\,\text{m}$, $\alpha = 2$, $\frac{d}{\lambda} = 0.5$, $\beta_0 = 30\,\text{dB}$, $\sigma^2 = -40\,\text{dBm}$.

Figure 3.6 shows the relationship between the minimum secrecy rate and the BS transmission power. Schemes 1 and 2 fix the UAV above user 1 and user 2, respectively, with optimized beamforming and RIS phase shifts, while Scheme 3 excludes RIS, relying on a direct link and BS-only beamforming. As BS power increases, so does the minimum secrecy rate, due to stronger received signals. The proposed scheme outperforms Schemes 1 and 2 by optimizing the UAV's position based on user and eavesdropper locations. Scheme 3 shows the weakest performance, highlighting the significant benefits of RIS in secure communications.

Figure 3.7 shows the relationship between the minimum secrecy rate and the number of RIS reflecting elements. It can be seen that as the number of RIS reflecting elements increases, the minimum secrecy rate of this system also increases. This is because the more RIS reflecting elements there are, the greater the array gain, which results in higher signal power at the receiver, thereby improving the minimum secrecy rate of the system. Additionally, it can be observed that the

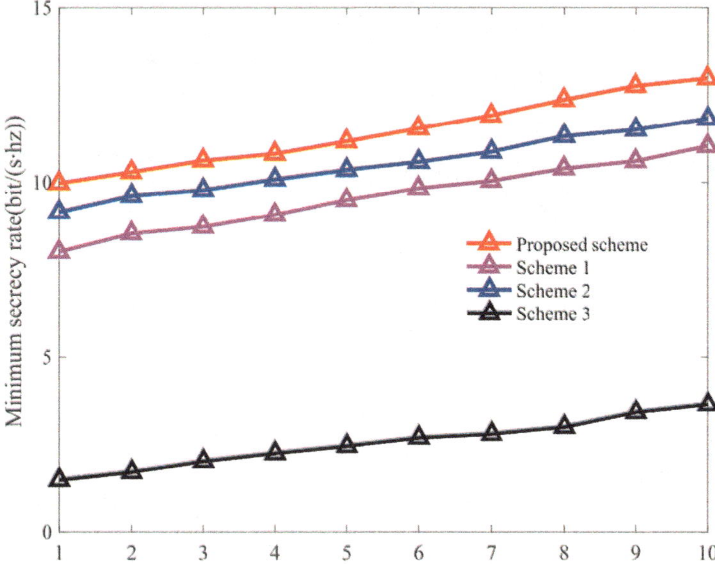

Fig. 3.6 Minimum secrecy rate versus P for different schemes

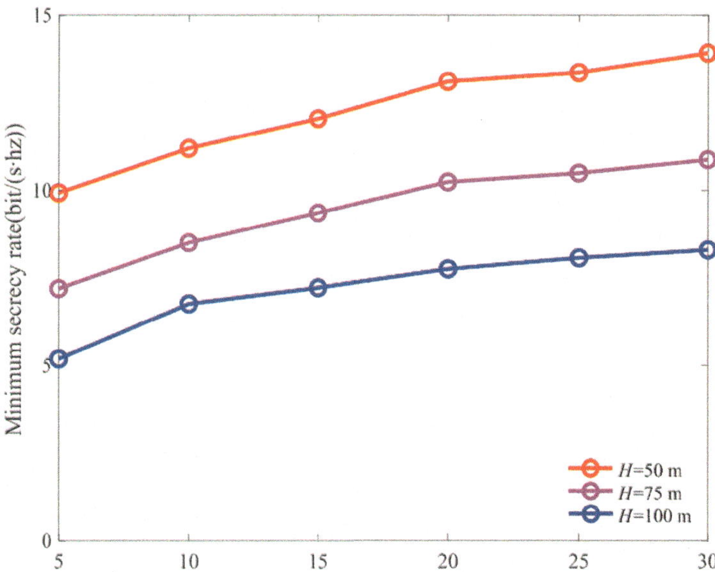

Fig. 3.7 Minimum secrecy rate versus N for different H

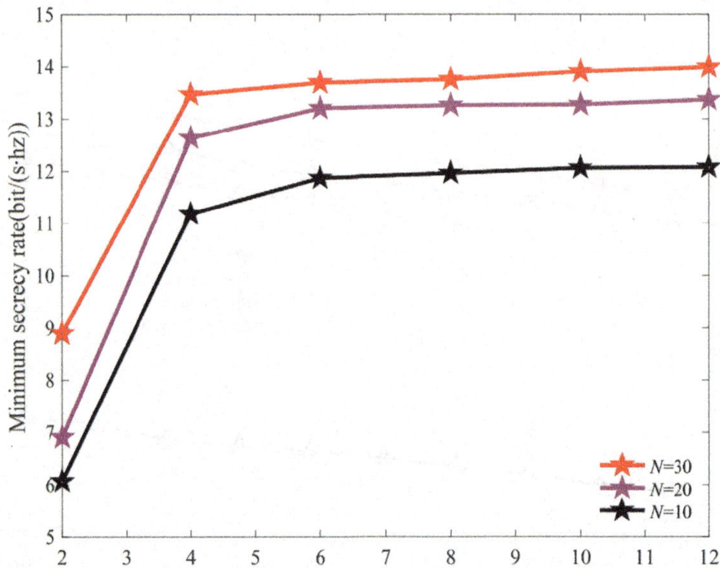

Fig. 3.8 Minimum secrecy rate versus M for different N

higher the UAV altitude, the lower the minimum secrecy rate. This is because a higher UAV altitude increases the path length of the air-to-ground channel, leading to greater path loss, which reduces the received power at the user.

Figure 3.8 illustrates that the minimum secrecy rate increases with the number of BS antennas, but the gain diminishes beyond a certain point. Initially, more antennas improve beamforming directionality, enhancing signal power at the RIS and users. However, due to the BS's fixed total transmit power, further antenna increases yield limited performance improvement once beamforming is sufficiently effective.

3.3.5 *Summary*

This section proposes a secure communication scheme for an AV-RIS-Relaying MEC system. By jointly optimizing the position of UAV, base station beamforming, and RIS phase shifts, the minimum secrecy rate of the system is maximized. The original problem is decomposed into several sub-problems, and methods such as first-order Taylor expansion are used to transform the original optimization problem into a convex optimization problem, which is solved using an alternating optimization algorithm. Simulation results verify the effectiveness and good convergence of the proposed scheme.

References

1. M. Li, N. Cheng, J. Gao, Y. Wang, L. Zhao, X. Shen, Energy-efficient UAV-assisted mobile edge computing: resource allocation and trajectory optimization. IEEE Trans. Veh. Technol. **69**(3), 3424–3438 (2020)
2. S. Bi, L. Huang, H. Wang, Y.-J.A. Zhang, Lyapunov-guided deep reinforcement learning for stable online computation offloading in mobile-edge computing networks. IEEE Trans. Wirel. Commun. **20**(11), 7519–7537 (2021)
3. B. Zhu, E. Bedeer, H.H. Nguyen, R. Barton, Z. Gao, UAV trajectory planning for AoI-minimal data collection in UAV-aided IoT networks by transformer. IEEE Trans. Wirel. Commun. **22**(2), 1343–1358 (2023)
4. Y. Ding, H. Han, W. Lu, Y. Wang, N. Zhao, X. Wang, X. Yang, DDQN-based trajectory and resource optimization for UAV-aided MEC secure communications. IEEE Trans. Veh. Technol. **73**(4), 6006–6011 (2024)
5. Y. Bian, J. Hu, P. Zhang, S. Wang, Y. Wang, J. Cong, C. Fu, Joint trajectory control, power control, and collection schedule in UAV-assisted anti-jamming wireless data collection with imperfect CSI. IEEE Commun. Lett. **28**(12), 2839–2843 (2024)
6. Y. Ding, Q. Zhang, W. Lu, N. Zhao, A. Nallanathan, X. Wang, X. Yang, Collaborative communication and computation for secure UAV-enabled MEC against active aerial eavesdropping. IEEE Trans. Wirel. Commun. **23**(11), 15915–15929 (2024)
7. Z. Han, T. Zhou, T. Xu, H. Hu, Joint user association and deployment optimization for delay-minimized UAV-aided MEC networks. IEEE Wirel. Commun. Lett. **12**(10), 1791–1795 (2023)
8. D. Wang, J. Tian, H. Zhang, D. Wu, Task offloading and trajectory scheduling for UAV-enabled MEC networks: an optimal transport theory perspective. IEEE Wirel. Commun. Lett. **11**(1), 150–154 (2022)
9. B. Liu, Y. Wan, F. Zhou, Q. Wu, R.Q. Hu, Resource allocation and trajectory design for MISO UAV-assisted MEC networks. IEEE Trans. Veh. Technol. **71**(5), 4933–4948 (2022)
10. Q. Wu, X. Guan, R. Zhang, Intelligent reflecting surface-aided wireless energy and information transmission: an overview. Proc. IEEE **110**(1), 150–170 (2022)
11. H. Shen, W. Xu, S. Gong, Z. He, C. Zhao, Secrecy rate maximization for intelligent reflecting surface assisted multi-antenna communications. IEEE Commun. Lett. **23**(9), 1488–1492 (2019)
12. H. Hu, Z. Sheng, A.A. Nasir, H. Yu, Y. Fang, Computation capacity maximization for UAV and RIS cooperative MEC system with NOMA. IEEE Commun. Lett. **28**(3), 592–596 (2024)
13. Y. Xu, T. Zhang, Y. Zou, Y. Liu, Reconfigurable intelligence surface aided UAV-MEC systems with NOMA. IEEE Commun. Lett. **26**(9), 2121–2125 (2022)
14. X. Qin, Z. Song, T. Hou, W. Yu, J. Wang, X. Sun, Joint optimization of resource allocation, phase shift, and UAV trajectory for energy-efficient RIS-assisted UAV-enabled MEC systems. IEEE Trans. Green Commun. Netw. **7**(4), 1778–1792 (2023)
15. S. Wang, X. Song, T. Song, Y. Yang, Fairness-aware computation offloading with trajectory optimization and phase-shift design in RIS-assisted multi-UAV MEC network. IEEE Internet Things J. **11**(11), 20547–20561 (2024)
16. H. Mei, K. Yang, J. Shen, Q. Liu, Joint trajectory-task-cache optimization with phase-shift design of RIS-assisted UAV for MEC. IEEE Wirel. Commun. Lett. **10**(7), 1586–1590 (2021)
17. P. Truong, T. do-Duy, A. Masaracchia, N. Vo, V. Phan, D. Ha, T. Duong, Computation offloading and resource allocation optimization for mobile edge computing-aided UAV-RIS communications. IEEE Access **12**, 107971–107983 (2024)
18. L. Li, W. Guan, C. Zhao, Y. Su, J. Huo, Trajectory planning, phase shift design, and IoT devices association in flying-RIS-assisted mobile edge computing. IEEE Internet Things J. **11**(1), 147–157 (2024)
19. Z. Zhai, X. Dai, B. Duo, X. Wang, X. Yuan, Energy-efficient UAV-mounted RIS assisted mobile edge computing. IEEE Wirel. Commun. Lett. **11**(12), 2507–2511 (2022)

20. Y. Liao, Y. Song, S. Xia, Y. Han, N. Xu, X. Zhai, Energy minimization of RIS-assisted cooperative UAV–USV MEC network. IEEE Internet Things J. **11**(20), 32490–32502 (2024)
21. B. Duo, M. He, Q. Wu, Z. Zhang, Joint dual-UAV trajectory and RIS design for ARIS-assisted aerial computing in IoT. IEEE Internet Things J. **10**(22), 19584–19594 (2023)
22. Y. Gu, Y. Ma, X. Wang, A. Shah, Security energy efficiency optimization and analysis of aerial-RIS-assisted UAV-MEC system. IEEE Access **12**, 118953–118967 (2024)
23. Y. Zhou, Z. Ma, G. Liu, Z. Zhang, P.L. Yeoh, B. Vucetic, Y. Li, Secure multi-layer MEC systems with UAV-enabled reconfigurable intelligent surface against full-duplex eavesdropper. IEEE Trans. Commun. **72**(3), 1565–1577 (2024)
24. E.T. Michailidis, M.-G. Volakaki, N.I. Miridakis, D. Vouyioukas, Optimization of secure computation efficiency in UAV-enabled RIS-assisted MEC-IoT networks with aerial and ground eavesdroppers. IEEE Trans. Commun. **72**(7), 3994–4009 (2024)
25. Y. Gao, Z. Wang, Y. Zhang, W. Lu, J. Tang, N. Zhao, F. Gao, Multi-IRS-aided secure communication in UAV-MEC networks. IEEE Trans. Veh. Technol. https://doi.org/10.1109/TVT.2025.3527586
26. S. Boyd, L.V. Andenberghe, *Convex Optimization* (Cambridge University Press, Cambridge, 2004)
27. B.R. Marks, G.P. Wright, A general inner approximation algorithm for nonconvex mathematical programs. Oper. Res. **26**, 681–683 (1978)
28. W. Lu, M. Cao, Y. Gao, J. Cao, Q. Hua, B. Li, N. Zhao, Secure communication method based on intelligent reflection surface assisted UAV relay system. J. Electron. Inf. Technol. **44**(7), 2273–2280 (2022)

Chapter 4
DRL-Based Secure Communications for UAV-Enabled MEC Systems

A secure communication scheme based on DRL in multi-UAV-MEC system is presented in this chapter for non-cooperative and cooperative task offloading schemes. In the proposed method, we first use the spiral placement algorithm to deploy the UAVs. Then we utilize DRL to enhance the system utility. The major contributions of this chapter are as follows:

- A secure communication model for multi-UAV-MEC system is proposed in this chapter. In the proposed scheme, we maximize the system utility for secure offloading, considering the limitations of the system secure performance, computing tolerable delay as well as energy consumption.
- In the proposed scheme, we formulate the long-term offloading process as a MDP, then subsequently develop both single-agent and multi-agent RL solutions to optimize system utility.
- Numerical results indicate the convergence of the offloading decision optimization scheme proposed in this chapter. In the proposed scheme, the multi-agent based scheme shows a more significant system utility than single-agent.

The rest of this chapter is organized as follows. Related studies are listed in Sect. 4.1. Then, we present two system models in Sect. 4.2.1. The optimization problems were illustrated in Sect. 4.2.2. We study the DRL-based single-agent scheme and multi-agent scheme, respectively in Sect. 4.2.3.

4.1 Related Studies

The 5G mobile communications has brought in a multitude of applications with high delay demands [1–3]. Many intelligent 5G mobile devices face energy limitations, and the substantial power consumption from intensive processes remains a critical issue [4–8]. To address these issues, the authors proposed MEC and offloading

W. Lu et al., *Secure Communications in Unmanned Aerial Vehicle-Enabled Mobile Edge Computing Systems*, SpringerBriefs in Computer Science,
https://doi.org/10.1007/978-981-96-9611-6_4

methods [9, 10]. By leveraging MEC, mobile users near the network edge can offload computational tasks to nearby servers, significantly lowering both energy usage and processing delay [11, 12].

Equipping UAVs with edge servers allows quick deployment since UAVs have high mobility and LoS transmission capabilities. Additionally, this significantly reduces energy consumption and delay during the computing process [13–15]. Under energy constraints, to optimize task migration efficiency under energy constraints, Li et al. employed UAV-mounted edge servers [16]. A UAV-MEC system including a UAV-MEC server was investigated by Zhang et al. to minimize the weighted task cost that both energy consumption and latency through optimal system offloading [17]. Li et al. minimize the UAV energy consumption through optimizing the flight trajectory as well as task offloading decisions [18]. In [19], Zhang et al. investigated a UAV-MEC system to minimize the energy consumption by jointly optimizing power allocation, time allocation, trajectory, etc. Zhang et al. employed UAVs as dual-function edge computing nodes and relay stations to reduce latency [20]. Dual-function proposed an optimization approach that concurrently adjusts UAV flight trajectory, resource allocation of the system as well as task offloading decisions to reduce energy consumption [21].

Since offloaded data is vulnerable to be eavesdropped via LoS links in the UAV-MEC system, ensuring the secure transmission of offloading data to the UAV for edge computing is of great significance. Jing et al. maximized the secure transmission rate of users by optimizing the flight trajectory in the UAV-MEC system based on DRL in [22]. Gu et al. achieved a reduction in energy consumption for both UAV computing and data offloading in [23]. Li et al. optimized the transmit power, task allocation as well as UAV trajectory to minimize the overall energy consumption of the UAV[24]. Focused on maximizing the secrecy capacity, Xu et al. further advance d this field by optimizing computation resources and flight trajectory in the UAV-assisted secure MEC system for both TDMA and NOMA as shown in [25]. Unlike stationary ground-based eavesdroppers addressed in prior studies, UAV-based eavesdroppers benefit from superior channel quality enabled by LoS links, making intercepted data more accessible. Key challenges in mitigating UAV eavesdroppers include addressing the unpredictability of their locations and ensuring collision avoidance among UAVs. With the goal of maximizing the minimum secrecy capacity, Han and Zhou proposed a comprehensive optimization framework that simultaneously adjusts the position of the UAV, user transmission power, task offloading proportions, and jamming power in scenarios involving UAV eavesdroppers in [26, 27].

Furthermore, it is challenging to apply traditional optimization techniques to several design problems in MEC networks, particularly offloading decision problems. DRL can manage complex and unpredictable decision-making issues, making it a potent tool for optimization in MEC networks. In [28], a UAV-MEC network was examined, where the offloading decision is optimized using DRL to enhance the computational performance. Lu et al. proposed an offloading decision optimization based on Dinkelbach-guided DRL to improve security calculation efficiency in a UAV-aided MEC network in [29]. Moreover, multi-agent deep reinforcement learning (MADRL) performs better than DRL for algorithm scalability and strategic complexity. In [30], the total delay and energy consumption of IoT devices in an MEC network were minimized by using MADRL. A MADRL-based algorithm was proposed to maximize energy efficiency in a MEC-enabled heterogeneous network in [31].

Our studies integrate the DRL and secure transmission to minimize the system utility and overall delay and In a multi-UAV assisted MEC network. We also consider the differences between user tasks that different types of tasks have different preference degrees for latency and the remaining energy of computing devices and the partial offloading from GUs to UAVs to further enhance the practicality of the proposed methods.

4.2 Secure Transmission for Non-cooperative Multi-UAV-MEC

4.2.1 System Model for Secure Transmission for Non-cooperative Multi-UAV-MEC

This section begins with a description of the system architecture, followed by the formulation of the secure communication framework. Subsequently, we examine both local and offloaded computation models.

4.2.1.1 System Model

In the proposed multi-UAV MEC framework shown in Fig. 4.1, one GJ, M UAVs functioning as edge servers (UAV_Ss), and K GUs form the legitimate network

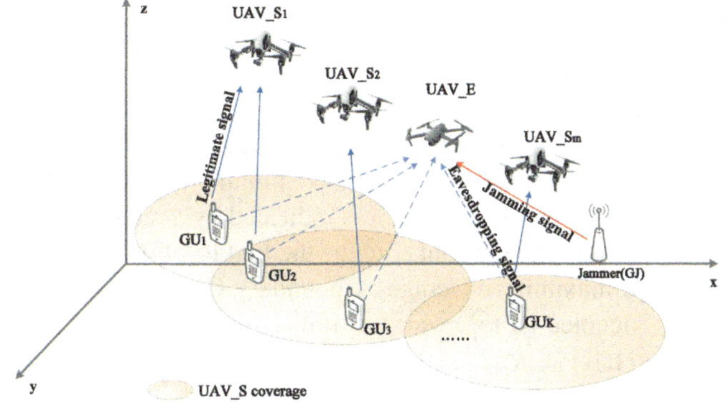

Fig. 4.1 A multi-UAV assisted MEC network

while a single UAV serving as an external eavesdropper (UAV_E). Prior research [25, 32] demonstrates that UAV_Ss can reconstruct and cancel the jamming signals of GJ through synthetic aperture radar processing. However, the absence of GJ signal information forces it to interpret jamming for UAV_E as part of the useful data stream, effectively reducing its eavesdropping accuracy.

In this chapter, a supposition is made that the positions of UAVs serving as edge servers (referred to as UAV_Ss), the eavesdropping UAV (UAV_E), GUs, and the GJ are fixed. The coordinates of the k-th GU ($k \in \mathcal{K}$, with $\mathcal{K} = \{1, 2, \ldots, K\}$) are designated as $w_k^{\mathrm{G}} = (x_k^{\mathrm{G}}, y_k^{\mathrm{G}}, 0)^{\mathrm{T}}$. The coordinates of the GJ are marked as $w_{\mathrm{J}} = (x_{\mathrm{J}}, y_{\mathrm{J}}, 0)^{\mathrm{T}}$. And the coordinates of the UAV_E are expressed as $w_{\mathrm{E}} = (x_{\mathrm{E}}, y_{\mathrm{E}}, h_{\mathrm{E}})^{\mathrm{T}}$, where h_{E} indicates the height of the UAV_E.For the m-th UAV_S ($m \in \mathcal{M}$, where $\mathcal{M} = \{1, 2, \ldots, M\}$), its coordinates are denoted by $w_m^{\mathrm{S}} = (x_m^{\mathrm{S}}, y_m^{\mathrm{S}}, h_m^{\mathrm{S}})^{\mathrm{T}}$, and h_m^{S} represents the height of this particular UAV_S$_m$. We consider all GUs associated with UAV_S$_m$ as $\mathcal{Z}_m = \{1, \ldots, Z_m\}$, their coordinates can be denoted as $w_{z_m}^{\mathrm{GS}} = (x_{z_m}^{\mathrm{GS}}, y_{z_m}^{\mathrm{GS}}, 0)^{\mathrm{T}}$. Additionally, it holds that $\sqrt{(x_{z_m}^{\mathrm{GS}} - x_m^{\mathrm{S}})^2 + (y_{z_m}^{\mathrm{GS}} - y_m^{\mathrm{S}})^2} \leq R$, where R signifies the coverage radius of UAV_S.It is taken into consideration that the UAV_E has a more excellent coverage ability compared to UAV_S.

The placement and quantity of UAV_Ss are determined by two key factors: the spatial distribution of GUs and the service radius of each UAV_S. The objective is to determine the minimum quantity of UAV_Ss needed to service all GUs, leading to the following problem formulation.

$$(\mathrm{P1}): \min_{w_m^{\mathrm{S}}} \quad M \tag{4.1a}$$

$$s.t. \quad \sqrt{\left(x_{z_m}^{\mathrm{GS}} - x_m^{\mathrm{S}}\right)^2 + \left(y_{z_m}^{\mathrm{GS}} - y_m^{\mathrm{S}}\right)^2} \leq R, \forall m, \tag{4.1b}$$

$$\mathcal{Z}_1 \cup \mathcal{Z}_2 \cup \ldots \cup \mathcal{Z}_M = \mathcal{K}, \tag{4.1c}$$

where constraint (4.1b) defines the maximum coverage capability of each UAV_S, while complete GU coverage is ensured through constraint (4.1c).

We employ the spiral placement algorithm to solve the aforementioned optimization problem as cited in [33]. The main concept is to place the UAVs functioning as edge servers (UAV_Ss) sequentially along the area perimeter. Specifically, we take Fig. 4.2 as an example to illustrate the steps of the spiral placement algorithm.

We randomly select a boundary GU$_{i_0}$ for positioning the first UAV acting as an edge server (UAV_S$_1$). For instance, GU$_3$ is indicated by a red triangular symbol in the bottom-left position. Then, we take $w_{i_0}^{\mathrm{G}}$ as the first location of UAV_S$_1$.

Subsequently, to maximize coverage of boundary GUs, we optimize the placement of UAV_S$_1$ denoted as w_1^{S}, which is initialized to w_3^{G}. At this juncture, we input w_1^{S}, the set $\{\mathrm{GU}_3\}$ as $\mathcal{K}_{\mathrm{prio}}$, and supplementary set $\mathcal{K}_{\mathrm{sec}}$ containing remaining uncovered GUS. The problem can be resolved by several algorithms as mentioned in [34, 35].

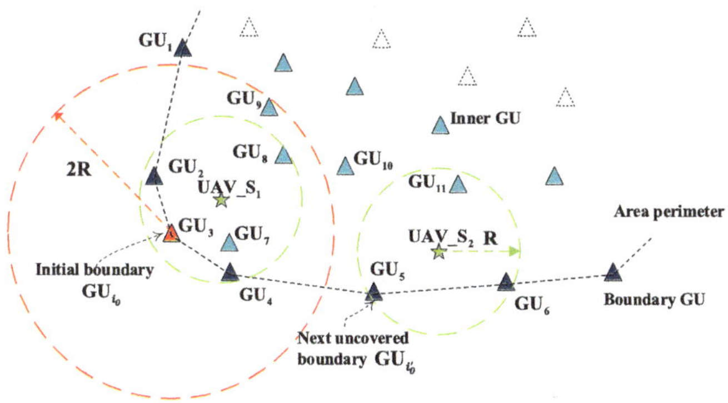

Fig. 4.2 Illustration of the spiral algorithm

After that, as shown in Fig. 4.2, the boundary GU_2 and GU_4 can be covered while maintaining coverage of GU_3.

Next, we extend coverage to maximize inclusion of inner GUs in a similar manner while ensuring that the boundary GU_2, GU_3, and GU_4 are covered first. Then we input the updated w_1^S, the set of uncovered inner GUs as $\mathcal{K}_{sec}$ and the set $\{GU_2, GU_3, GU_4\}$ as $\mathcal{K}_{prio}$.

Following this phase, both GU_7 and GU_8 is successfully covered, and the algorithm marks UAV_S$_1$'s terminal position with a green pentagram symbol (Fig. 4.2).

For UAV_S$_2$ deployment, the algorithm initializes at the first unserved boundary GU (GU_5) adjacent to GU_4 in the counterclockwise direction, then applies the established placement procedure to determine its optimal position. This iterative procedure continues until complete GU coverage is achieved.

4.2.1.2 Secure Communication Model

Adopting the free-space propagation model, the channel gain for the GU$_k$-UAV_S$_m$ link is

$$h_{k,m} = \frac{\mu}{d_{k,m}^2}, \tag{4.2}$$

where μ is the channel gain at the reference distance of 1 m, and $d_{k,m} = \sqrt{\left(x_k^G - x_m^S\right)^2 + \left(y_k^G - y_m^S\right)^2 + h_m^{S\,2}}$ is the distance between the GU$_k$ and UAV_S$_m$.

Additionally, the channel gain for the GU$_k$-UAV_E link is

$$h_{k,e} = \frac{\mu}{d_{k,e}^2}, \tag{4.3}$$

where $d_{k,e} = \sqrt{\left(x_k^{\mathrm{G}} - x_{\mathrm{E}}\right)^2 + \left(y_k^{\mathrm{G}} - y_{\mathrm{E}}\right)^2 + {h_{\mathrm{E}}}^2}$ is the distance between the GU$_k$ and UAV_E.

The channel gain for the GJ-UAV_E link is

$$h_{j,e} = \frac{\mu}{d_{j,e}^2}, \tag{4.4}$$

where $d_{j,e} = \sqrt{(x_{\mathrm{J}} - x_{\mathrm{E}})^2 + (y_{\mathrm{J}} - y_{\mathrm{E}})^2 + {h_{\mathrm{E}}}^2}$ is the distance between the GJ and UAV_E.

Supposing that a set of M non-overlapping channels are allocated to the UAVs acting as edge servers (UAV_Ss) for gathering task data from the GUs, where GUs utilize TDMA as mentioned in [36].

Consequently, the SNR of the received signals from GU$_k$ to UAV_S$_m$ is provided by

$$r_{k,m} = \frac{h_{k,m} p_k}{\delta_m^2}, \forall k, m, \tag{4.5}$$

where p_k is the transmit power of GU$_k$, and δ_m^2 is the AWGN at UAV_S$_m$.

Since UAV_E fails to differentiate between the signals transmitted by GU$_k$ and GJ, the SINR of the received signals from the GU$_k$ to UAV_E can be given by

$$r_{k,e} = \frac{h_{k,e} p_k}{h_{j,e} p_j + \delta_e^2}, \forall k, \tag{4.6}$$

where p_j is the transmit power of GJ, and δ_e^2 is the AWGN at UAV_E.

Thus, the task offloading rate from the GU$_k$ to UAV_S$_m$ is

$$R_{k,m} = \log_2\left(1 + \frac{h_{k,m} p_k}{\delta_m^2}\right), \forall k, m. \tag{4.7}$$

The eavesdropping rate from the GU$_k$ to UAV_E is

$$R_{k,e} = \log_2\left(1 + \frac{h_{k,e} p_k}{h_{j,e} p_j + \delta_e^2}\right), \forall k. \tag{4.8}$$

Finally, the secure offloading rate from the GU$_k$ to UAV_S$_m$ is

$$R_{k,m}^{\text{sec}} = \left(R_{k,m} - R_{k,e}\right)^{+}, \forall k. \tag{4.9}$$

4.2.1.3 Computation Model

Consider a system where each GU processes a specific task type denoted as $\mathcal{G} = \{1, 2, \ldots, G\}$. The corresponding task L_k^g for GU$_k$ is characterized by the tuple $L_k^g \triangleq (D_g, T_g)$, representing data volume and timing constraints. Here, D_g represents the data size of task type g, and T_g represents the maximum tolerable latency for task type g. GUs have the option to process their type g tasks either locally or through task offloading to an accessible UAV that functions as an edge server (UAV_S) for processing.

(1) Local Computing When GU$_k$ selects local processing for task L_k^g, the associated delay $T_{k,g}^{\text{local}}$ represents the exclusive computational latency by the CPU of GU$_k$. Then, $T_{k,g}^{\text{local}}$ is

$$T_{k,g}^{\text{local}} = \frac{D_g C^{\text{local}}}{f_k^{\text{local}}}, \forall k, \tag{4.10}$$

where C^{local} the CPU cycles per bit needed for local task processing, while f_k^{local} denotes the computing capacity of the GU$_k$'s CPU.

Given GU$_k$'s effective capacitance coefficient q_k, the local computing energy consumption is expressed as

$$E_{k,g}^{\text{local}} = q_k T_{k,g}^{\text{local}} \left(f_k^{\text{local}}\right)^3, \forall k. \tag{4.11}$$

(2) Offloading Computing When GU$_k$ offloads its task to UAV_S$_m$, the process comprises three sequential phases.

First, GU$_k$ transmits the task data to the UAV_S$_m$ with the corresponding transmission delay for L_k^g is given by

$$T_{k,g,m}^{\text{tran}} = \frac{D_g}{W_m R_{k,m}^{\text{sec}}}, \forall k, m, \tag{4.12}$$

where W_m is the bandwidth of the GU$_k$.

During the computation phase, UAV_S$_m$ processes the received task data. The execution time for L_k^g at the UAV_S$_m$ is

$$T_{k,g,m}^{\text{comp}} = \frac{D_g C_m}{f_m}, \forall k, m, \tag{4.13}$$

where C_m is the number of CPU cycles required by the UAV_S$_m$ to compute one bit of task, and f_m is the computing capacity of UAV_S$_m$.

Given UAV_S$_m$'s effective capacitance p_m, its computation energy consumption is formulated as

$$E_{k,g,m}^{\text{comp}} = p_m T_{k,g,m}^{\text{comp}} (f_m)^3, \forall k, m. \tag{4.14}$$

In the third stage, the UAV acting as an edge server (UAV_S$_m$) delivers the task to the GU$_k$. Because UAV_S's transmission power is stronger than that of GU, the significantly reduced size of processed results compared to input data, the corresponding transmission delay becomes negligible as noted in [23].

Consequently, the total processing latency for offloaded task L_k^g can be estimated as

$$T_{k,g}^m \approx T_{k,g,m}^{\text{tran}} + T_{k,g,m}^{\text{comp}}, \forall k, m. \tag{4.15}$$

Thus the execution delay of task L_k^g is

$$T_{k,g} = \begin{cases} T_{k,g}^{\text{local}}, & \text{local computing} \\ T_{k,g}^m, & \text{offloading to UAV\_S}_m \end{cases}, \tag{4.16}$$

where $T_{k,g}$ should meet the constraint $T_{k,g} \leq T_g$. The total delay for overall tasks is $\sum_{k=1}^{K} T_{k,g}$.

The offloading decision of task L_k^g for the GU$_k$ is given as $\boldsymbol{a}_g^k = \left[a_0^{g,k}, a_1^{g,k}, a_2^{g,k}, \ldots, a_M^{g,k}\right]$, the binary indicator $a_0^{g,k} = 1$ signifies local computation by GU$_k$, while $a_m^{g,k} = 1$ denotes task offloading to UAV_S$_m$ subject to the constraint of $\sum_{i=0}^{M} a_i^{g,k} = 1, a_i^{g,k} \in \{0, 1\}$.

4.2.2 Problem Formulation

The formulation of the system utility function and the corresponding optimization problem is formulated in this section. In case of local task execution at GU$_k$, these utility measures take the following form:

$$U_{k,g}^{\text{local,de}} = \frac{T_g - T_{k,g}^{\text{local}}}{T_g}, \tag{4.17}$$

$$U_{k,g}^{\text{local,en}} = \frac{E_{\max}^g - E_{k,g}^{\text{local}}}{E_{\max}^g}, \tag{4.18}$$

respectively, where $E_{\max}^{g}$ is the maximum usable energy of the GU_k with task L_k^g. When task offloading occurs to UAV_S$_m$, the acquired utilities for both latency and energy consumption are expressed as

$$U_{k,g,m}^{\mathrm{de}} = \frac{T_g - T_{k,g}^{m}}{T_g}, \tag{4.19}$$

$$U_{k,g,m}^{\mathrm{en}} = \frac{E_{\max}^{\mathrm{UAV\_S}} - \sum_{i \in O_{k,m}} E_{i,g,m}^{\mathrm{comp}}}{E_{\max}^{\mathrm{UAV\_S}}}, \tag{4.20}$$

respectively, where $E_{\max}^{\mathrm{UAV\_S}}$ denotes the energy capacity limit for UAV_S$_m$ while $O_{k,m} = \{1, 2, \ldots, O_{k,m}\}$ represents the queue of GUs that previously offloaded tasks to the UAV_S$_m$ prior to GU_k.

The system utility function can be expressed as

$$\begin{aligned} U^{\mathrm{sys}} = & \sum_{k=1}^{K} \left[\theta_g \left(a_0^{g,k} U_{k,g}^{\mathrm{local,de}} + \sum_{m=1}^{M} a_m^{g,k} U_{k,g,m}^{\mathrm{de}} \right) \right] \\ & + \sum_{k=1}^{K} \left[\eta_g \left(a_0^{g,k} U_{k,g}^{\mathrm{local,en}} + \sum_{m=1}^{M} a_m^{g,k} U_{k,g,m}^{\mathrm{en}} \right) \right], \end{aligned} \tag{4.21}$$

where θ_g and η_g respectively characterize task L_k^g sensitivity to processing delay and device energy status.

Following UAV_S development optimization, we maximize system utility through offloading decision vector $\boldsymbol{a}_g^k$ in the following formulation

$$(\mathrm{P2}): \quad \max_{\boldsymbol{a}_g^k} \quad U^{\mathrm{sys}} \tag{4.22a}$$

$$s.t. \quad \sum_{i=0}^{M} a_i^{g,k} = 1, a_i^{g,k} \in \{0, 1\}, \forall k, \tag{4.22b}$$

$$T_{k,g} \le T_g, \forall k, \tag{4.22c}$$

$$R_{k,m}^{\mathrm{sec}} \ge R_{\min}^{\mathrm{sec}}, \forall k, m, \tag{4.22d}$$

$$E_{\max}^{\mathrm{UAV\_S}} \ge \sum_{i \in O_{k,m}} E_{i,g,m}^{\mathrm{comp}}, \forall k, m, \tag{4.22e}$$

$$E_{\max}^{g} \ge E_{k,g}^{\mathrm{local}}, \forall k, \tag{4.22f}$$

where constraint (4.22b) signifies that the task can either be entirely computed locally or completely offloaded to UAVs acting as edge servers (UAV_Ss) for computation. The latency requirement in constraint (4.22c) bounds task L_k^g's processing time by T_g. Constraint (4.22d) maintains communication security by enforcing $R_{\min}^{\mathrm{sec}}$ as the minimum acceptable secure offloading rate. For energy limitations, constraint (4.22e) restricts each UAV_S's computational energy consumption below $E_{\max}^{\mathrm{UAV\_S}}$, while constraint (4.22f) caps local computation energy at $E_{\max}^g$ per task.

The optimization problem presented in (4.22a) is non-convex in nature and failed To be resolved utilizing traditional schemes. Therefore, in this chapter, schemes based on single-agent and multi-agent reinforcement learning (RL) are used to address this problem. Related details are provided in the next section.

4.2.3 Problem Solution

For developing secure offloading framework, we model the sequential decision-making process as a MDP. First, we present the core MDP components, then propose a single-agent scheme based on RL for maximizing system utility.

4.2.3.1 Basic Elements of MDP

The MDP framework comprises four core components: state space, action space, transition dynamics, and reward function. Given that GUs can only observe environmental states without prior knowledge, we model the offloading process as a transition probability-free MDP. The key elements are formally defined below.

(1) State Since UAV_Ss' fluctuating energy reserves directly impact the system utility, the system state can be denoted by $S = \{UST_1, UST_2, \ldots, UST_M\}$, where UST_m is the quantitative value of $U_{k,g,m}^{\mathrm{en}}$, which is carried out according to Table 4.1, and there are a total of four quantization levels as mentioned in [37].

The system utility function in (4.21) can be rewritten as

$$\begin{aligned} U^{\mathrm{sys}'} =& \sum_{k=1}^{K}\left[\theta_g\left(a_0^{g,k}U_{k,g}^{\mathrm{local,de}} + \sum_{m=1}^{M} a_m^{g,k} U_{k,g,m}^{\mathrm{de}}\right)\right] \\ &+ \sum_{k=1}^{K}\left[\eta_g\left(a_0^{g,k}U_{k,g}^{\mathrm{local,en}} + \sum_{m=1}^{M} a_m^{g,k} \frac{UST_m - 1}{3}\right)\right]. \end{aligned} \tag{4.23}$$

Table 4.1 The residual energy ratio of UAV_S

$U_{k,g,m}^{\mathrm{en}}$	(0.00, 0.25)	(0.25, 0.50)	(0.50, 0.75)	(0.75, 1.00)
UST_m	1	2	3	4

Thus, the optimization problem is transformed into

$$\max_{\boldsymbol{a}_g^k} \quad U^{\text{sys}'} \tag{4.24}$$

$$s.t. \quad 1 \leq UST_m \leq 4, \forall k, m. \tag{4.25}$$

$$\text{(4.22b)–(4.22d), (4.22f),}$$

(2) Action For task L_k^g, the current action is encoded in the offloading decision vector $\boldsymbol{a}_g^k$.

(3) Reward Function For task L_k^g, the agent's instantaneous reward following action $\boldsymbol{a}_g^k$ implementation is

$$r_g^k = \begin{cases} \theta_g U_{k,g}^{\text{local,de}} + \eta_g U_{k,g}^{\text{local,en}} & a_0^{g,k} = 1 \\ \theta_g U_{k,g,m}^{\text{de}} + \eta_g \frac{UST_m - 1}{3}, & a_m^{g,k} = 1 \end{cases}. \tag{4.26}$$

4.2.3.2 Single-Agent Scheme Based on QL

Q-learning (QL), a foundational RL algorithm, operates through iterative Q-table construction. The agent selects actions according to Q-value estimates representing discounted future rewards. At each step t, the agent observes the current state s_t and executes the action $\boldsymbol{a}_t$. The environment then provides an immediate reward $r(s_t, a_t)$ and transitions to the next state s_{t+1}. The agent updates its Q-value in Q-table according to the reward $r(s_t, a_t)$, which is

$$\begin{aligned} Q\left(s_{t+1}, \boldsymbol{a}_{t+1}\right) = (1-\alpha)\, Q\left(s_t, \boldsymbol{a}_t\right) + \alpha \left[r\left(s_t, \boldsymbol{a}_t\right)\right. \\ \left. +\gamma \max Q\left(s_{t+1}, \boldsymbol{a}'\right)\right], \end{aligned} \tag{4.27}$$

where $Q\left(s_t, \boldsymbol{a}_t\right)$ and $r\left(s_t, \boldsymbol{a}_t\right)$ denotes the Q-value and immediate reward after taking action $\boldsymbol{a}_t$ under s_t, respectively. s_{t+1} is the next state after taking action $\boldsymbol{a}_t$, $\max Q\left(s_{t+1}, \boldsymbol{a}'\right)$ is the max Q-value in the state s_{t+1} according the Q-table. $\alpha \in [0, 1)$ is the learning rate and $\gamma \in [0, 1)$ is the discount factor.

Next, we propose a QL-based single-agent task offloading scheme. Firstly, all GUs collectively function as a unified agent, with their computational tasks organized in a processing queue. During each decision interval, the agent employs an ε-greedy policy which explores random actions with probability ε and exploits Q-table knowledge with probability $1 - \varepsilon$. During Q-table-guided decision-making, the agent prioritizes the maximum Q-value action (Eq. (4.27)). When constraints prevent this selection, it defaults to the feasible action offering the highest immediate reward. Subsequent to action execution, the agent calculates state transitions and rewards, performs Q-table updates, and triggers environmental state progression.

4.2.4 Multi-Agent Scheme Based on RL

Given the diversity in task requirements, a MADRL system is implemented to enhance secure offloading performance.

4.2.4.1 Multi-Agent Scheme Based on NQL

As a multi-agent reinforcement learning method, Nash Q-learning (NQL) defines agent g's Q-value function $Q_g(s, \boldsymbol{a}_1, \boldsymbol{a}_2, \ldots, \boldsymbol{a}_G)$ to aggregate current and future rewards. The corresponding Nash Q-function of agent g is given by

$$\begin{aligned} Q_g^*\left(s, \boldsymbol{a}_1, \boldsymbol{a}_2, \ldots, \boldsymbol{a}_G\right) =& r_g\left(s, \boldsymbol{a}_1, \boldsymbol{a}_2, \ldots, \boldsymbol{a}_G\right)+ \\ & \gamma \sum_{s' \in S} p\left(s' | s, \boldsymbol{a}_1, \boldsymbol{a}_2, \ldots, \boldsymbol{a}_G\right) V_g\left(s', \pi_1^*, \pi_2^*, \ldots, \pi_G^*\right), \end{aligned} \tag{4.28}$$

where $r_g(s, \boldsymbol{a}_1, \boldsymbol{a}_2, \ldots, \boldsymbol{a}_G)$ represents the immediate reward that agent g obtains when performing $\boldsymbol{a}_g$ in state s under the joint actions $(\boldsymbol{a}_1, \boldsymbol{a}_2, \ldots, \boldsymbol{a}_G)$. γ denotes the discount factor, S represents the complete state space, and $p(s'|s, \boldsymbol{a}_1, \boldsymbol{a}_2, \ldots, \boldsymbol{a}_G)$ characterizes state evolution under joint actions. Nash equilibrium strategies $(\pi_1^*, \pi_2^*, \ldots, \pi_G^*)$ determine the value function $V_g(s', \pi_1^*, \pi_2^*, \ldots, \pi_G^*)$ representing agent g's cumulative discounted rewards in state s' when all agents adhere to Nash policies.

The Q-values of the agent is continuously updated by the NQL algorithm from interacting with the environment. Based on the observed state s, the coordinate actions $(\boldsymbol{a}_1, \boldsymbol{a}_2, \ldots, \boldsymbol{a}_G)$ are simultaneously executed by the agent collective. The environment then transitions to state s', requiring each agent to monitor the collective actions and rewards across all agents. Q-values is updated by agent g via

$$\begin{aligned} Q_{t+1}^g\left(s, \boldsymbol{a}_1, \boldsymbol{a}_2, \ldots, \boldsymbol{a}_G\right) =& (1-\alpha)\, Q_t^g\left(s, \boldsymbol{a}_1, \boldsymbol{a}_2, \ldots, \boldsymbol{a}_G\right)+ \\ & \alpha\left[r_t^g\left(s, \boldsymbol{a}_1, \boldsymbol{a}_2, \ldots, \boldsymbol{a}_G\right)+\gamma Nash Q_t^g\left(s'\right)\right], \end{aligned} \tag{4.29}$$

where α is the learning rate, while $Nash Q_t^g(s')$ denotes agent g's Nash equilibrium reward in state s', formally expressed as

$$Nash Q_t^g\left(s'\right)=\pi_1\left(s'\right) \cdots \pi_G\left(s'\right) \cdot Q_t^g\left(s'\right). \tag{4.30}$$

To compute $Nash Q_t^g(s')$, the agent g requires simultaneous access to all Q-functions $Q_t^1, \cdots, Q_t^G$, necessitating the maintenance of G Q-tables per agent. Following the approach In (4.29), the agent g updates its Q-value estimate for agent

j via

$$Q_{t+1}^{j}\left(s, \boldsymbol{a}_1, \boldsymbol{a}_2, \ldots, \boldsymbol{a}_G\right) = (1-\alpha)\, Q_t^{j}\left(s, \boldsymbol{a}_1, \boldsymbol{a}_2, \ldots, \boldsymbol{a}_G\right) + \alpha\left[r_t^{j}\left(s, \boldsymbol{a}_1, \boldsymbol{a}_2, \ldots, \boldsymbol{a}_G\right) + \gamma Nash Q_t^{j}\left(s'\right)\right]. \tag{4.31}$$

We introduce a NQL-based multi-agent task offloading scheme, where each agent's queue length reflects the count of GUs sharing identical task types. The queue length set $\{L_1, L_2, \ldots, L_G\}$ formally represents this system state. For the multi-agent framework, the state computation remains consistent with the single-agent case, but introduces distinct action and reward formulations.

(1) Action The current action for agent g handling task L_k^g is denoted as $\boldsymbol{a}_g^k$.

(2) Reward Function Upon processing L_k^g, the instantaneous reward for agent g's action $\boldsymbol{a}_g^k$ follows (4.26). Adopting the conventional ε-greedy policy, the multi-agent scheme may encounter situations where no joint action meets both Nash equilibrium requirements and operational constraints. In such scenarios, priority is given to constraint-compliant actions with optimal immediate returns.

4.2.5 Simulation Results

In the simulation, 30 GUs are randomly distributed within an area of 300×300 m^2. The coordinates of UAV_E and the ground junction (GJ) are fixed at $(131, 114, 50)^T$ meters and $(131, 114, 0)^T$ meters respectively. In the multi-agent scheme, there are three types of tasks. The multi-agent system comprises 3 agents handling 10 tasks each. Task-dependent parameters are documented in Table 4.2. The algorithm employs a learning rate $\alpha = 0.01$ and discount factor $\gamma = 0.8$, with an exploration probability that linearly decreases from 1 to 0.01 and the decay step size being 40 episodes.

Figure 4.3 illustrates the optimized placement of UAV_Ss, with their locations indicated by green pentagram markers and numbered sequentially. The

Table 4.2 Parameter settings varying by task types

	Type 1	Type 2	Type 3
Data size (Mbit)	40	15	2
Maximum usable energy of GU (J)	25.00	9.38	1.25
Maximum latency tolerance (s)	0.50	0.20	0.05
Preference for residual energy	0.1	0.2	0.5
Preference for delay	0.8	0.4	0.2

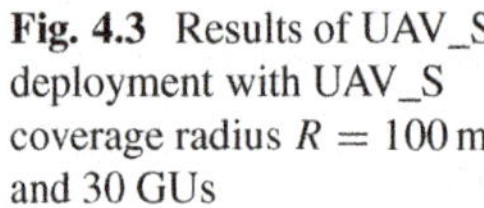

Fig. 4.3 Results of UAV_S deployment with UAV_S coverage radius $R = 100\,\text{m}$ and 30 GUs

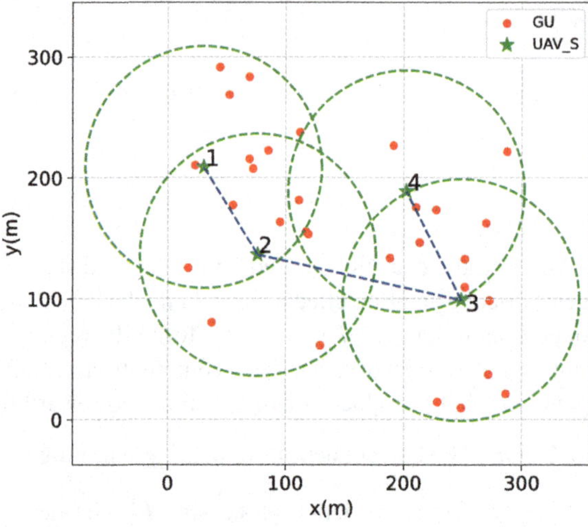

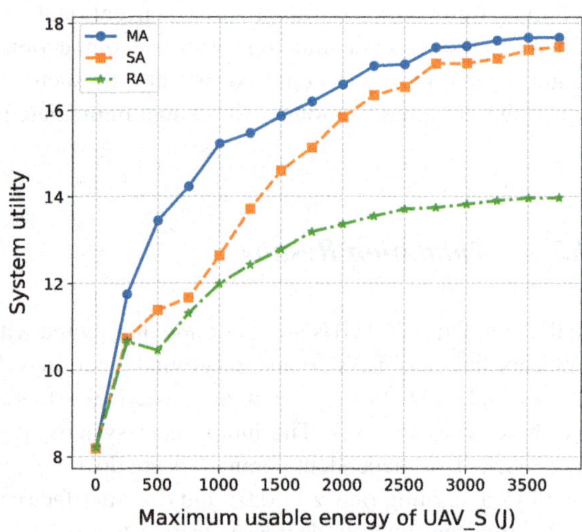

Fig. 4.4 The system utility versus $E_{\text{max}}^{\text{UAV\_S}}$

configuration requires four UAV_Ss, whose interconnecting blue lines form an underdeveloped spiral pattern due to the limited number of nodes. However, this spiral shape isn't very distinct due to the relatively small number of UAV_Ss.

Our security-enhanced SA and MA schemes are evaluated against a non-learning RA baseline where actions are randomly chosen from feasible options in Figs. 4.4, 4.5, 4.6, and 4.7, highlighting the superior computational security performance.

Figure 4.4 demonstrates the correlation between system utility and UAV_S energy capacity $E_{\text{max}}^{\text{UAV\_S}}$. Results indicate the multi-agent (MA) approach outperforms both single-agent (SA) and random offloading (RA) methods, as MA's Nash equilibrium-based optimization effectively manages inter-task competition for optimal offloading decisions.

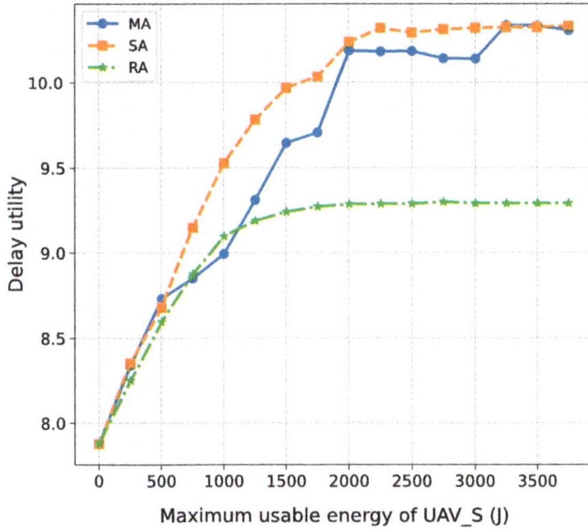

Fig. 4.5 The delay utility versus $E_{\max}^{\text{UAV\_S}}$

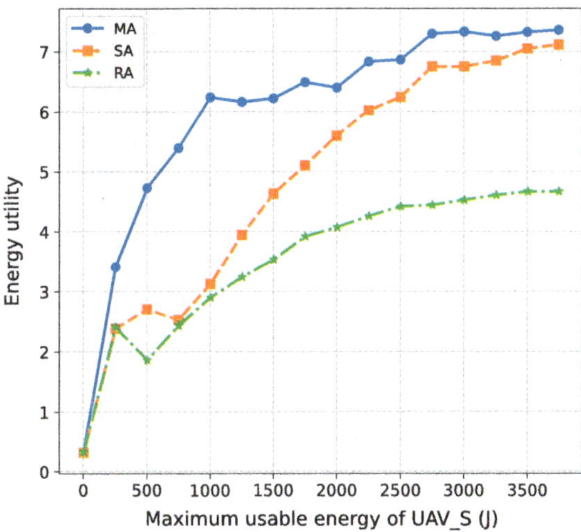

Fig. 4.6 The energy utility versus $E_{\max}^{\text{UAV\_S}}$

Figure 4.4 illustrates the relationship between the system utility and the maximum usable energy of UAVs acting as edge servers (UAV_S), denoted as $E_{\max}^{\text{UAV\_S}}$. As depicted in Fig. 4.4, it can be observed that the multi-agent (MA) scheme performs better than the single-agent (SA) and random offloading (RA) schemes. The reason for this is that the MA scheme takes into account the competition among the three types of tasks and thus achieves the optimal offloading strategy in accordance with Nash equilibrium. As shown in Fig. 4.4, the system utility improves with increasing values of $E_{\max}^{\text{UAV\_S}}$. This trend primarily stems from the growing number of offloaded tasks before $E_{\max}^{\text{UAV\_S}}$ reaches 3000 J. However, once $E_{\max}^{\text{UAV\_S}}$ exceeds this threshold, the system utilities under both the MA and SA schemes begin to level off. The stabilization occurs because, with ample energy supply, the

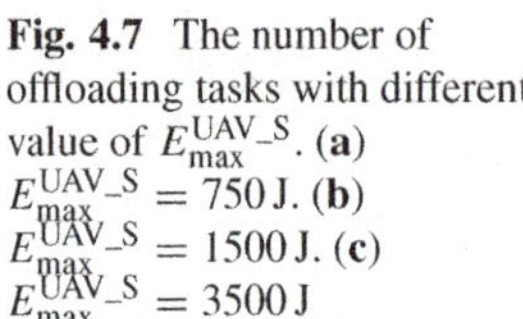

Fig. 4.7 The number of offloading tasks with different value of $E_{\max}^{\mathrm{UAV\_S}}$. (**a**) $E_{\max}^{\mathrm{UAV\_S}} = 750\,\mathrm{J}$. (**b**) $E_{\max}^{\mathrm{UAV\_S}} = 1500\,\mathrm{J}$. (**c**) $E_{\max}^{\mathrm{UAV\_S}} = 3500\,\mathrm{J}$

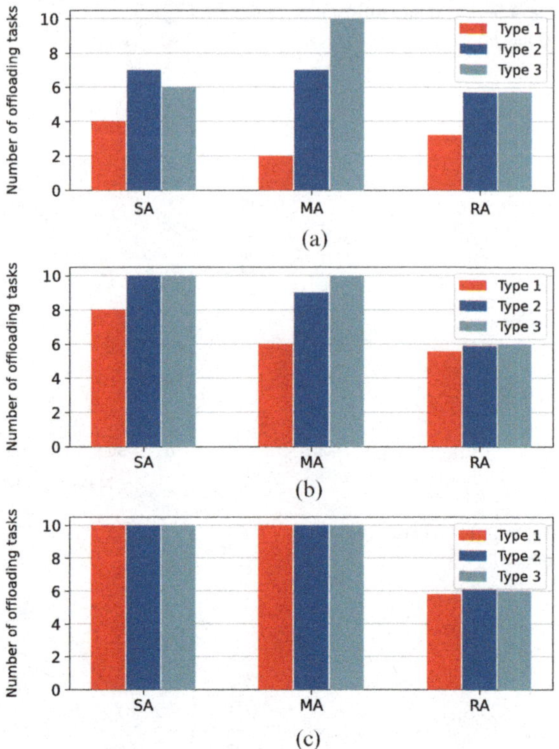

likelihood of a task being selected for offloading computation approaches certainty (nearly 100%).

Figure 4.5 illustrates how delay utility varies with UAV_S energy capacity $E_{\max}^{\mathrm{UAV\_S}}$. The MA scheme achieves intermediate delay utility between SA (highest) and RA (lowest). This occurs because single-agent decisions typically favor higher-utility offloading, while multi-agent coordination requires compromise. Notably, when $E_{\max}^{\mathrm{UAV\_S}}$ exceeds 3000 J, both MA and schemes shift to near-complete task offloading.

Figure 4.6 illustrates the relationship between energy utility and UAV_S energy capacity $E_{\max}^{\mathrm{UAV\_S}}$. The MA scheme maintains superior energy efficiency compared to both SA and RA methods, owing to its optimized task offloading mechanism that minimizes computational overhead and preserves residual energy.

Figure 4.7 presents the task offloading distribution across different schemes as a function of UAV_S energy capacity $E_{\max}^{\mathrm{UAV\_S}}$. Analysis of Fig. 4.7a indicates MA's preference for energy-efficient Type 3 tasks over energy-intensive Type 1 tasks, contrasting with SA's behavior. This strategic resource allocation maximizes system efficiency under energy constraints. Figure 4.7b illustrates MA's superior energy utilization at 1500 J through selective offloading of both Type 1 and 2 tasks, while RA shows limited scalability. The final Fig. 4.7c demonstrates full offloading capability achieved by both MA and SA approaches.

Here's a refined and paraphrased version of your paragraph with improved academic flow and reduced redundancy:

Figure 4.7 presents the comparative analysis of offloaded tasks across different schemes under varying $E_{\max}^{\text{UAV\_S}}$ values. As illustrated in Fig. 4.7a, the MA scheme processes fewer Type 1 tasks but more Type 3 tasks compared to the SA approach. This discrepancy arises from the substantially higher computational energy demand of Type 1 tasks. By prioritizing Type 3 task offloading, the MA scheme achieves greater system utility under limited energy budgets $E_{\max}^{\text{UAV\_S}}$. Figure 4.7b reveals that at $E_{\max}^{\text{UAV\_S}} = 1500$ J, the MA scheme offloads fewer Type 1 and Type 2 tasks than the SA scheme, resulting in enhanced energy efficiency. In contrast, the RA scheme exhibits performance saturation due to its unoptimized task allocation. Finally, Fig. 4.7c demonstrates complete offloading to UAV_Ss in both MA and SA schemes, indicating energy-sufficient conditions where all tasks are processed remotely.

Figure 4.8 illustrates the system utility evolution during the learning process under MA and SA schemes, with UAV_S's maximum usable energy $E_{\max}^{\text{UAV\_S}}$ set at 1500 J. The results demonstrate three key observations: First, during the initial 20,000 episodes, the system utility exhibits rapid growth accompanied by significant fluctuations. Second, beyond this threshold, the utility stabilizes within a bounded range, confirming the convergence of both approaches. Third, comparative analysis reveals the MA scheme ultimately achieves higher system utility than its SA counterpart.

Figure 4.9 presents the comparative analysis of total delay between MA and SA schemes during the learning process. The delay initially decreases with training episodes before eventually stabilizing, with the MA scheme exhibiting a higher

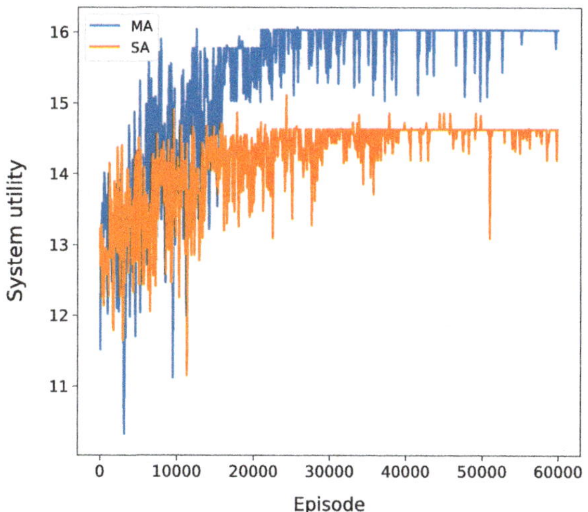

Fig. 4.8 The system utility during the learning process using the MA and SA schemes

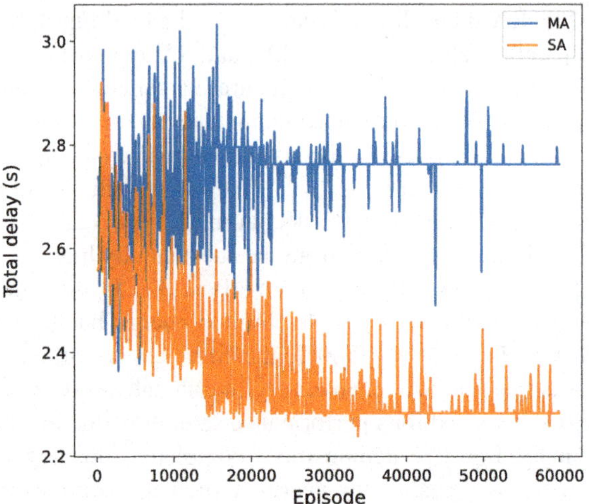

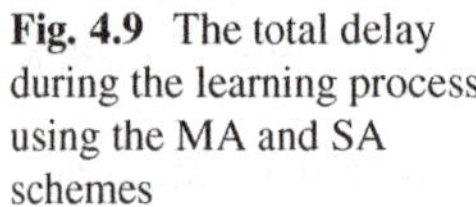
Fig. 4.9 The total delay during the learning process using the MA and SA schemes

final delay compared to the SA approach. This difference stems from the MA scheme's selective offloading strategy which processes fewer tasks than the SA method, where more extensive task offloading leads to lower overall latency since offloading computation consistently outperforms local computing in terms of delay. However, this apparent advantage in delay reduction comes at the cost of energy efficiency—while the SA scheme achieves lower delay, the MA approach demonstrates superior energy utility by preserving more residual UAV_S energy through its optimized offloading decisions. This fundamental trade-off between delay performance and energy conservation explains why the SA scheme's reduced latency does not translate to greater system utility, as its aggressive offloading strategy significantly depletes available energy resources, ultimately compromising overall system performance.

Figure 4.10 compares the normalized energy consumption of four UAV_Ss between MA and SA schemes, where normalized consumption represents the ratio of actual energy used to the maximum available energy $E_{\max}^{\mathrm{UAV\_S}}$. The analysis reveals that the SA scheme consistently exhibits higher energy consumption across all UAV_Ss because it processes more offloading tasks. This increased energy expenditure directly reduces the system's energy utility while simultaneously improving its delay performance. Figure 4.11 further examines the final energy consumption patterns, showing that neighboring UAV_Ss demonstrate similar energy utilization levels. The balanced energy distribution achieved by the MA scheme contributes to its superior energy efficiency compared to the SA approach.

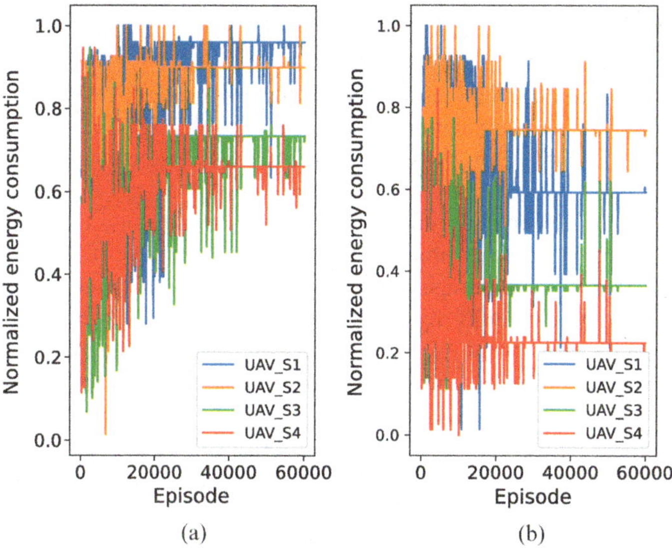

Fig. 4.10 The normalized energy consumption of four UAV_Ss during the learning process using the (**b**) MA and (**a**) SA schemes

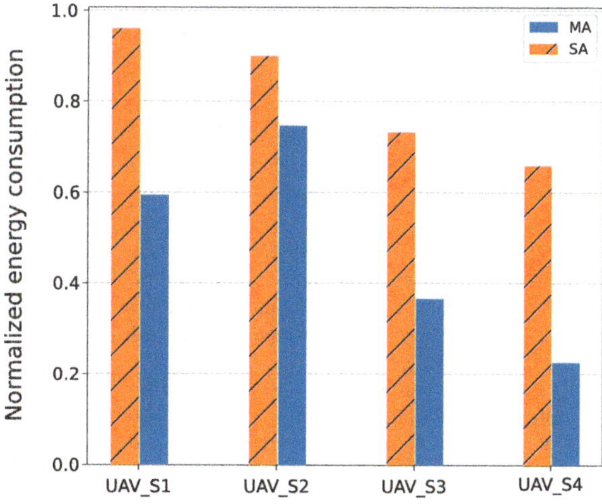

Fig. 4.11 The final normalized energy consumption using the MA and SA schemes

4.2.6 Summary

This paper proposes a secure transmission framework for multi-UAV-MEC systems, where UAV_Ss deliver computational services to GUs through LoS communication channels. To enhance security, a GJ is employed to transmit interference signals targeting UAV_E.

The system implementation involves three key components: First, an efficient spiral placement algorithm minimizes the required number of UAV_Ss while ensuring complete user coverage. Second, we establish an optimization problem that maximizes system utility by jointly considering computational latency and device residual energy. Third, we develop reinforcement learning-based solutions, including both single-agent and multi-agent approaches, to determine optimal secure offloading strategies.

Comparative simulations reveal the superior performance of the multi-agent scheme over both the single-agent approach and random offloading strategy in terms of overall system efficiency. The proposed solution demonstrates significant improvements in balancing energy consumption, delay reduction, and security maintenance.

References

1. M. Shafi, A.F. Molisch, P.J. Smith, T. Haustein, P. Zhu, P. De Silva, F. Tufvesson, A. Benjebbour, G. Wunder, 5G: a tutorial overview of standards, trials, challenges, deployment, and practice. IEEE J. Sel. Areas Commun. **35**(6), 1201–1221 (2017)
2. Z. Xiong, Y. Zhang, D. Niyato, R. Deng, P. Wang, L. Wang, Deep reinforcement learning for mobile 5G and beyond: fundamentals, applications, and challenges. IEEE Veh. Techonol. Mag. **14**(2), 44–52 (2019)
3. Z. Zhou, X. Chen, E. Li, L. Zeng, K. Luo, J. Zhang, Edge intelligence: paving the last mile of artificial intelligence with edge computing. Proc. IEEE **107**(8), 1738–1762 (2019)
4. J. Kang, Z. Xiong, X. Li, Y. Zhang, D. Niyato, C. Leung, C. Miao, Optimizing task assignment for reliable blockchain-empowered federated edge learning. IEEE Trans. Veh. Technol. **70**(2), 1910–1923 (2021)
5. X. Foukas, G. Patounas, A. Elmokashfi, M.K. Marina, Network slicing in 5G: survey and challenges. IEEE Commun. Mag. **55**(5), 94–100 (2017)
6. Z. Xiong, Y. Zhang, W.Y.B. Lim, J. Kang, D. Niyato, C. Leung, C. Miao, UAV-assisted wireless energy and data transfer with deep reinforcement learning. IEEE Trans. Cogn. Commun. Netw. **7**(1), 85–99 (2021)
7. H. Yang, A. Alphones, Z. Xiong, D. Niyato, J. Zhao, K. Wu, Artificial-intelligence-enabled intelligent 6G networks. IEEE Netw. **34**(6), 272–280 (2020)
8. H. Yang, Z. Xiong, J. Zhao, D. Niyato, C. Yuen, R. Deng, Deep reinforcement learning based massive access management for ultra-reliable low-latency communications. IEEE Trans. Wirel. Commun. **20**(5), 2977–2990 (2021)
9. X. Chen, L. Jiao, W. Li, X. Fu, Efficient multi-user computation offloading for mobile-edge cloud computing. IEEE/ACM Trans. Netw. **24**(5), 2795–2808 (2016)
10. J. Cao, W. Feng, N. Ge, J. Lu, Delay characterization of mobile edge computing for 6G time-sensitive services. IEEE Internet Things J. **8**(5), 3758–3773 (2021)

11. H. Ma, Z. Zhou, X. Chen, Leveraging the power of prediction: predictive service placement for latency-sensitive mobile edge computing. IEEE Trans. Wirel. Commun. **19**(10), 6454–6468 (2020)
12. S. Yu, X. Chen, Z. Zhou, X. Gong, D. Wu, When deep reinforcement learning meets federated learning: intelligent multitimescale resource management for multiaccess edge computing in 5G ultradense network. IEEE Internet Things J. **8**(4), 2238–2251 (2021)
13. X. Pang, M. Sheng, N. Zhao, J. Tang, D. Niyato, K. Wong, When UAV meets IRS: expanding air-ground networks via passive reflection. IEEE Wirel. Commun. **28**(5), 164–170 (2021)
14. H. Yang, J. Zhao, Z. Xiong, K.-Y. Lam, S. Sun, L. Xiao, Privacy-preserving federated learning for UAV-enabled networks: learning-based joint scheduling and resource management. IEEE J. Sel. Areas Commun. **39**(10), 3144–3159 (2021)
15. L. Qian, W. Wu, W. Lu, Y. Wu, B. Lin, T.Q.S. Quek, Secrecy based energy-efficient mobile edge computing via cooperative non-orthogonal multiple access transmission. IEEE Trans. Wirel. Commun. **69**(7), 4659–4677 (2021)
16. J. Li, Q. Liu, P. Wu, F. Shu, S. Jin, Task offloading for UAV-based mobile edge computing via deep reinforcement learning, in *2018 IEEE/CIC International Conference on Communications in China (ICCC)* (2018), pp. 798–802
17. K. Zhang, X. Gui, D. Ren, D. Li, Energy-latency tradeoff for computation offloading in UAV-assisted multiaccess edge computing system. IEEE Internet Things J. **8**(8), 6709–6719 (2021)
18. Y. Liu, K. Xiong, Q. Ni, P. Fan, K.B. Letaief, UAV-assisted wireless powered cooperative mobile edge computing: joint offloading, CPU control, and trajectory optimization. IEEE Internet Things J. **7**(4), 2777–2790 (2020)
19. T. Zhang, Y. Xu, J. Loo, D. Yang, L. Xiao, Joint computation and communication design for UAV-assisted mobile edge computing in IoT. IEEE Trans. Ind. Inform. **16**(8), 5505–5516 (2020)
20. L. Zhang, N. Ansari, Latency-aware IoT service provisioning in UAV-aided mobile-edge computing networks. IEEE Internet Things J. **7**(10), 10573–10580 (2020)
21. Y.K. Tun, Y.M. Park, N.H. Tran, W. Saad, S.R. Pandey, C.S. Hong, Energy-efficient resource management in UAV-assisted mobile edge computing. IEEE Commun. Lett. **25**(1), 249–253 (2021)
22. L. Jing, X. Jia, Y. Lv, N. Wan, Maximizing the average secrecy rate for UAV-assisted MEC: a DRL method, in *2021 IEEE 5th Advanced Information Technology, Electronic and Automation Control Conference (IAEAC)* (2021), pp. 2514–2518
23. X. Gu, G. Zhang, J. Gu, Offloading optimization for energy-minimization secure UAV-edge-computing systems, in *2021 IEEE Wireless Communications and Networking Conference (WCNC)* (2021), pp. 1–6
24. Y. Li, Y. Fang, L. Qiu, Joint computation offloading and communication design for secure UAV-enabled MEC systems, in *2021 IEEE Wireless Communications and Networking Conference (WCNC)* (2021), pp. 1–6
25. Y. Xu, T. Zhang, D. Yang, Y. Liu, M. Tao, Joint resource and trajectory optimization for security in UAV-assisted MEC systems. IEEE Trans. Wirel. Commun. **69**(1), 573–588 (2021)
26. D. Han, T. Shi, Secrecy capacity maximization for a UAV-assisted MEC system. China Commun. **17**(10), 64–81 (2020)
27. Y. Zhou, C. Pan, P.L. Yeoh, K. Wang, M. Elkashlan, B. Vucetic, Y. Li, Secure communications for UAV-enabled mobile edge computing systems. IEEE Trans. Wirel. Commun. **68**(1), 376–388 (2020)
28. D. Sha, R. Zhao, DRL-based task offloading and resource allocation in multi-UAV-MEC network with SDN, in *2021 IEEE/CIC International Conference on Communications in China (ICCC)* (2021), pp. 595–600
29. W. Lu, Y. Ding, Y. Feng, G. Huang, N. Zhao, A. Nallanathan, Dinkelbach-guided deep reinforcement learning for secure communication in UAV-aided MEC networks, in *GLOBECOM 2022 - 2022 IEEE Global Communications Conference* (2022), pp. 1740–1745

30. F. Jiang, L. Dong, K. Wang, K. Yang, C. Pan, Distributed resource scheduling for large-scale MEC systems: a multiagent ensemble deep reinforcement learning with imitation acceleration. IEEE Internet Things J. **9**(9), 6597–6610 (2022)
31. Y. Xiao, Y. Song, J. Liu, Towards energy efficient resource allocation: when green mobile edge computing meets multi-agent deep reinforcement learning, in *ICC 2022 - IEEE International Conference on Communications* (2022), pp. 4056–4061
32. W. Lu, Y. Ding, Y. Gao, S. Hu, Y. Wu, N. Zhao, Y. Gong, Resource and trajectory optimization for secure communications in dual-UAV-MEC systems. IEEE Trans. Ind. Inform. **18**(4), 2704–2713 (2022)
33. J. Lyu, Y. Zeng, R. Zhang, T.J. Lim, Placement optimization of UAV-mounted mobile base stations. IEEE Commun. Lett. **21**(3), 604–607 (2017)
34. N. Megiddo, Linear-time algorithms for linear programming in R3 and related problems. SIAM J. Comput. **12**(4), 759–776 (1983)
35. J. Elzinga, D.W. Hearn, Geometrical solutions for some minimax location problems. Transp. Sci. **6**(4), 379–394 (1972)
36. S. Sun, G. Zhang, H. Mei, K. Wang, K. Yang, Optimizing multi-UAV deployment in 3D space to minimize task completion time in UAV-enabled mobile edge computing systems. IEEE Commun. Lett. **25**(2), 579–583 (2021)
37. X. Wang, X. Su, B. Liu, A novel network selection approach in 5G heterogeneous networks using Q-learning, in *2019 26th International Conference on Telecommunications (ICT)* (2019), pp. 309–313

Chapter 5
Conclusions and Future Directions

In this chapter, we summarize the brief and outlines potential directions for future research.

5.1 Conclusions

In this brief, we focus on the secure communication in the UAV-enabled MEC systems, and explores various secure communication schemes to enhance the security, efficiency, and adaptability of the system. Through a series of theoretical analyses, algorithm designs, and simulation verifications, we summarize this brief with the following conclusive remarks.

- PLS techniques make use of the inherent features of communication channels and transmission methods to ensure robust security in data transmission for UAV-enabled MEC systems. The key feature of PLS technology is that it provides high-quality secure communication by intelligently utilizing wireless channels as well as transmission methods. Furthermore, two secure communication schemes for the UAV-enabled MEC system under TDMA and NOMA transmission are proposed to enhance the secure communication performance of the system.
- RIS-based secure communication can further improve communication and computation efficiency in UAV-enabled MEC systems. Consisting of numerous reflecting elements, RISs are capable of dynamically adjusting the phase and amplitude of reflected signals, which can not only improve communication quality, but also assist in reducing the signal deterioration brought about by obstacles. Through considering two RIS-based UAV-enabled MEC systems for secure communication, we have performed simulation results to show the superiority of the RIS-based UAV-enabled MEC systems compared to the benchmarks.

W. Lu et al., *Secure Communications in Unmanned Aerial Vehicle-Enabled Mobile Edge Computing Systems*, SpringerBriefs in Computer Science,
https://doi.org/10.1007/978-981-96-9611-6_5

- DRL-based secure communication is an efficient method to address task offloading problems in UAV-enabled MEC systems. Thanks to its capability of handling complex and unpredictable decision-making problems in dynamic MEC scenarios, DRL can provide a real-time solution through interacting with the UAV-enabled MEC environment. Hence, a DRL-based secure communication scheme are proposed in this brief to maximize system utility or minimize time delay by optimizing task offloading decisions. We have performed extensive numerical results to show that DRL secure communication scheme outperforms the random offloading approach by a significant margin.

5.2 Future Directions

This brief presents the results on online optimization techniques for real time resource management in the field of secure communications for dynamic UAV-enabled MEC systems while ensuring security. The research presented in the following chapters opens up several interesting directions for further research, two of which are particularly promising and are illustrated as follows. Optimization of Secure Communications in the Context of Multi-Technology Integration: With the continuous development of communication technologies, UAV-enabled MEC systems in the future will be integrated with more emerging technologies, such as 6G, artificial intelligence (AI), blockchain, and so on. Investigating how to further optimize secure communication strategies in these integrated scenarios will be an important research direction. For example, by combining the high data rate and low latency characteristics of 6G with the intelligent decision-making ability of AI, more efficient and intelligent secure communication resource allocation and trajectory optimization can be achieved. Leveraging the decentralized characteristic of blockchain can enhance data security and privacy protection, ensuring that the secure communication performance of UAV-enabled MEC systems is further improved in complex environments with multiple users and nodes. Cross-layer Security Design and Optimization: Current research mostly focuses on single-layer security design, such as physical layer security or network layer security. In the future, cross-layer security design can be considered, comprehensively taking into account the security requirements and characteristics of multiple layers, including the physical layer, link layer, and network layer, for joint optimization. Through cross-layer design, the advantages of each layer can be fully utilized to achieve more comprehensive and efficient security protection. For example, beamforming technology can be used in the physical layer to improve signal confidentiality, reliable transmission protocols can be adopted in the link layer to ensure data integrity and correctness, and access control and encryption technologies can be utilized in the network layer to guarantee data security. Through cross-layer collaborative optimization, the overall security performance of the UAV-MEC system can be enhanced.

Made in the USA
Monee, IL
03 May 2026

49438517R00063